The Moosewood Cookbook

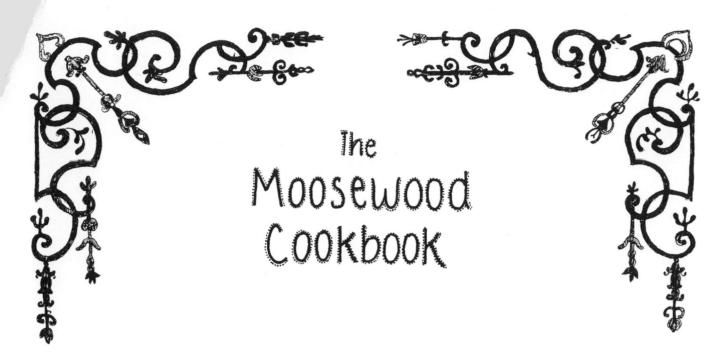

The
Moosewood
Cookbook

by Mollie Katzen

Ten Speed Press

Berkeley

In Memorium:
PHIL WOOD
(1938 - 2010)
Ten Speed Press founder;
godfather of this book.

 Dedicated to Hal, with love and gratitude.

Published in the United States by Ten Speed Press, an imprint of the Crown
Publishing Group, a division of Random House, LLC, a Penguin Random
House Company, New York.
www.crownpublishing.com
www.tenspeed.com

Ten Speed Press and the Ten Speed Press colophon are registered trademarks
of Random House LLC.

A version of this work was first published in 1974 by Mollie Katzen in Ithaca, New York.

Subsequent editions were published in the United States by Ten Speed Press, Berkeley,
in 1977, 1992, and 2000

Library of Congress Cataloging-in-Publication Data

Katzen, Mollie, 1950 -
    The Moosewood cookbook / Mollie Katzen. — 40th anniversary edition.
        pages cm
1. Vegetarian cooking. 2 Cooking (Natural foods) 3. Moosewood Restaurant
I. Moosewood Restaurant II. Title.
    TX837. M67 2014
    641.5'636 — dc23

Hardcover ISBN: 978-1-60774-756-7
Trade paperback ISBN: 978-1-60774-739-0

Printed in China

Cover design for original Ten Speed Press edition Meredith Barchat and Mollie Katzen
Revised cover design: Fifth Street Design, Nancy Austin, Mollie Katzen, and Chloe Rawlins
Illustrations. Mollie Katzen
Author photo for this edition: Lisa Keating

10 9 8 7 6 5 4

Revised edition

❧ Contents ❧

INTRODUCTION

Welcome to the Moosewood Cookbook

(From the first Ten Speed Press edition)

This book presents an adaptation-for-home-use of the cuisine of Moosewood Restaurant, in Ithaca, New York. The ideas for these recipes originated in the homes and imaginations of the many people who cook and have cooked there over the years.

Moosewood is the focal point to which each cook has brought her or his personal culinary heritage from family and friends. (Many grandmothers' recipes are featured.) Cooking styles are shared and traded at the restaurant. Moosewood's cooks also frequent the library, to read about the foods of other cultures. The result is an eclectic cuisine, with vegetarian and ethnic emphases, using the freshest ingredients available.

I was one of the founding members of Moosewood Restaurant, and I cooked there for 4½ years. During that time, in response to customers' requests, I adapted many Moosewood recipes, reducing them to a smaller yield, testing them at home for discriminating friends. Here is a compilation of the results. I hope you enjoy using this book as much as I enjoyed putting it together.

Mollie Katzen
Ithaca, New York
1977

❧ A History of This Book ❧

The Moosewood Cookbook grew, in part, out of a looseleaf binder filled with random notes intended to help keep track of what we were cooking in the tiny kitchen of our modest 1970s restaurant. With neither chef nor set menu, we were a group of friends (none of us culinary professionals) taking turns in the kitchen, cooking heartfelt versions of the food we loved, beginning with family favorites. We were also greatly inspired by international dishes as remembered from various world travels (actual or via the "ethnic restaurant" route), discovering cuisines from other countries that placed far less emphasis on meat and more on creative preparation of garden- and orchard-sourced ingredients. And indeed, what we served was deeply plant-based, although that term was not yet in anyone's vocabulary.

Our largely vegetarian framework had no particular dogma. We cooked simply and with passion, cheerfully pushing back on the traditional American dinner plate of the 1950s and '60s — the model that fed our childhoods. Now in our young adulthood, we wanted to redefine and self-define, and this was a perfect arena in which to do so. The food, prepared with a loving and sincere effort and minimal preciousness, spoke for itself. Our experimentation with whole grains, legumes, and fresh fruits and vegetables was enthusiastic, and it was also nonlinear. The book was an attempt to more or less standardize our "cuisine," which was varied and eclectic and often quite spontaneous — determined largely by the produce delivery of the day and the imagination and skill level of the cook. We had a casual approach to everything (including the idea of standardization itself), so, ideally, this would help us keep things somewhat consistent.

Our customers were not necessarily vegetarians - they simply wanted good food that tasted homemade and real. They also wanted to be able to replicate what we were making in their own kitchens. Requests for recipes became routine, and I regularly found myself sitting down after a shift, jotting down approximations of the dishes in. Eventually, I put together a series of pages, combining these after-shift notations with material from my own personal illustrated recipe journals. Backing from a neighboring independent bookstore ("McBooks") afforded the photocopying of a few hundred copies, which were then hand-collated and bound with plastic spiral spines, one at a time. Eight hundred copies of the resulting booklet sold out in a week. Second and third printings totaled another four thousand or so copies that sold out over the next year. Meanwhile, I had begun receiving unofficial mail orders - apparently from people who had passed through town, picked up a copy, and shared it with friends elsewhere. I was running to the post office a lot, and boxes of the booklets lived in the back of my car. It was seat-of-the-pants publishing all the way.

Enter Ten Speed Press, a then barely-known publishing company in Berkeley, California, that, at the time, was really just one guy with a vision and an apartment office. His name was Phil Wood, and he was looking for homespun, self-published projects to launch nationally. Phil encouraged me to expand the booklet, offering complete editorial and artistic autonomy, with two stipulations: that the narrative remain fresh, personal, and hand-lettered — and a promise that, no matter what I did, I would "keep the eggplant" (illustration on page 150 - still there!). And so I added more recipes, neatened up the hand-lettering, made new drawings, and upgraded, more or less, the communication of ingredients and instructions. In the fall of 1977, the Ten Speed Press edition of the Moosewood Cookbook - the one many people have come to know - was first published. It was not an overnight sensation by any means (contrary to some lore) but actually took a few years to catch on and begin to sell. Phil stuck with it throughout, keeping the book in print and in constant distribution. To this day — 40 years after the original spiral-bound booklet - the Moosewood Cookbook has never been out of print.

Fifteen years in, I decided to re-cook my way through the book, cover to cover. I wanted to see if I still agreed with the recipes or if the vegetarian zeitgeist had changed enough to merit revision. Many of the recipes remained essentially the same, and quite a few benefitted from lightening up, especially regarding dairy ingredients. I made small changes here and there, aiming for a more straightforward and sophisticated take on richness, flavor, layering, and texture. I also added about 25 new recipes, reflecting a growing sense of seasoning, and utilizing the broader selection of good produce that had (and has still, since then) become more widely available. The goal was to evolve the book but not change its essential character. This revised edition has been in circulation since 1992, and it's the one you will discover in the pages to come.

For Moosewood Cookbook's 40th birthday, Ten Speed Press and I have collaborated on an upgraded package with a fresh, new look that's built to last. Those of you with old, stained, dog-eared, scotch-taped, rubber-banded (and in some cases, coverless) copies of yesteryear might appreciate this newly refreshed edition — or perhaps it's for someone new to this tome. In any and every case, we are thrilled to celebrate this milestone with you! We hope these recipes — and this approach to cooking in general — will give you a range of ideas to play with and enjoy — and that the knowledge, comfort, and pleasures of a plant-based cuisine will continue to deepen for everyone.

Mollie Katzen
Kensington, California
2014

❧ PANTRY NOTES ☙

In case you need a brief explanation of some of the ingredients used in this book:

BEANS & LEGUMES: Usually these recipes call for dry beans to be soaked and cooked. Occasionally, it's fine to substitute canned — individual recipes will indicate this. When you use dry beans or legumes, save money by buying in bulk.

BUTTER: Use unsalted or lightly salted.

FOOD FROM CANS OR JARS: These recipes use very few canned (or jarred) foods, with the following exceptions: artichoke hearts or crowns, beans or chick peas (on occasion), water chestnuts, pineapple-in-juice, and tomato products (paste, purée, whole tomatoes, etc.)

DAIRY PRODUCTS: You can use lowfat (and often nonfat) everything: milk, cottage cheese, ricotta, sour cream, evaporated milk, yogurt, etc. Soy or rice milk can frequently be substituted.

EXTRACTS (VANILLA, ALMOND, ETC.): Use pure only.

FLOURS: Unless otherwise specified, use unbleached white flour.

FROZEN FOODS: I frequently tested these recipes with frozen unsweetened fruit (berries, cherries, etc.) with great success, when fresh were unavailable. You can also use frozen peas, corn, cooked squash, and if you're in a pinch, a 10-oz. package of frozen chopped spinach can substitute for 1 large bunch fresh in cooked dishes. Defrost and drain thoroughly before using.

GARLIC: Use fresh only and buy it frequently. The fresher, the better.

HERBS: If it's not specified, the recipe was tested with dried herbs, as these are more readily available year-round. However, if you have access to fresh herbs, by all means use them! Here's the exchange rate: 1 tsp. dried approximately equals 1 Tbs. minced fresh.

JUICES: Use fresh-squeezed lemon, lime, or orange juice in these recipes whenever possible.

OILS: Extra virgin olive oil is best for just about any savory destination. Exceptions are noted in individual recipes. As much as possible, store all oils away from excessive heat and light.

NUTS, SEEDS, NUT BUTTERS: Use unprocessed, available (often in bulk) at natural foods stores and at many grocery stores. Tahini (raw sesame paste) is available in natural foods stores, in some specialty groceries, and in the imported foods section of many grocery stores.

PASTA: The recipes in this book were tested with dried egg pasta of various shapes, but you can also use fresh. More details are on p. 75.

RICE: Short- and long-grain brown rice are interchangeable in these recipes. There is no nutritional difference, and the cooking method is the same. Short-grain is chewier; long-grain is fluffier. Buy either kind in bulk at natural foods stores.

SOY SAUCE: Japanese soy sauces (tamari or shoyu) have a deeper, slightly sweeter flavor than Chinese, which are thinner and saltier (and sometimes contain additives, so read the label). Whichever kind you prefer, you can find good soy sauce in natural foods stores and in Asian markets.

SWEETENERS: To varying degrees, sugar, brown sugar, honey, and real maple syrup are used in the desserts. In some cases they are interchangeable. This is indicated on individual recipes.

TOFU: Tofu is soybean curd, available in many forms. It is high in protein, low in price, and has no cholesterol. Buy it by the pound, packed in water in little plastic tubs, by the piece—out of large buckets of water, or vacuum-packed—either in plastic wrapping or in small boxes (see p. 91). Tofu is available in natural foods stores, in Asian markets, or in the produce department of the grocery store.

☆☆☆☆☆☆☆☆☆☆☆☆☆☆☆☆☆☆☆☆☆☆☆☆☆☆
SOME USEFUL TOOLS (HIGHLY RECOMMENDED)
☆☆☆☆☆☆☆☆☆☆☆☆☆☆☆☆☆☆☆☆☆☆☆☆☆☆

☆FOOD PROCESSOR~ for puréeing, grating, mincing, and mashing. For pie crusts, too. This time- and skin-saving device might turn out to be one of the best kitchen investments you'll ever make!

☆BLENDER~ It still does some things better than a food processor—it makes smoother purées and is good for processing medium-sized amounts.

☆MINI-PROCESSOR~ finely minces garlic and fresh herbs in seconds flat. It has about a 1-cup capacity.

☆CITRUS SQUEEZER~ manual or electric.

☆CUTTING BOARDS~ one for fruit, one for vegetables, and one for onions and garlic.

☆MICROWAVE OVEN~ for reheating with little or no cleanup. With a microwave, you'll be encouraged to do more cooking in advance.

☆ELECTRIC MIXER~ hand-held or larger. This is a must for baking, especially when beaten egg whites are featured.

☆WIRE WHISKS~ of varying sizes.

☆BOWLS~ of varying sizes.

☆SEVERAL COLANDERS~ including one big enough for pasta.

☆A FEW KNIVES THAT YOU JUST LOVE~ straight-edged and serrated, of various sizes, all of them very sharp.

☆SEVERAL SPOONS THAT YOU JUST LOVE~ including a large slotted one.

☆A SOUP POT ~ (kettle or Dutch oven)

☆A LARGE PASTA-BOILING POT

☆A LARGE (10- to 12-inch) SKILLET ~ for sautéing. Nonstick = ideal.

☆A MEDIUM TO LARGE WOK ~ for stir-fries. Nonstick, if possible.

☆A 6- TO 8-INCH CRÊPE OR OMELET PAN ~ Again, nonstick, if possible.

☆ SEVERAL SAUCEPANS WITH LIDS ~ various sizes.

☆ A TIMER WITH A BELL ~ So you can think about other things in the meantime.

☆A GARLIC PRESS (optional) ~ I actually prefer to mince garlic in a mini-processor or on a cutting board with a sharp paring knife, but some people love to press their garlic.

☆ BAKING PANS AND CASSEROLES ~ of various shapes and sizes.

☆TONGS ~ (useful for spaghetti); PASTA SCOOP ~ (useful for other shapes)

☆SPATULAS ~ metal and rubber.

☆ ROLLING PIN

☆ "WAFFLE" ~ heat absorber, to place under pots for very slow simmering.

☆ VEGETABLE SCRUB BRUSH and /or PEELER

☆ VEGETABLE STEAMER ~ a little metal basket to fit into a saucepan, letting you cook vegetables over water.

☆ OVEN THERMOMETER ~ to help ensure the success of your baking.

✳ TABLE OF CONVERSIONS ✳

✳ DRY INGREDIENTS ✳

Beans (any type): ½ cup = 100 grams
Cornmeal, coarse (polenta): 1 cup = 170 grams
Cornmeal, fine: 1 cup = 150 grams
Herbs, dried = ¼ to ⅓ the amount of fresh herbs
Flour, white unbleached: 1 cup = 140 grams
Grains, dried (rice, bulgur, wheat berries, etc.): 1 cup = 200 grams
Sugar, brown: 1 cup (packed) = 200 grams
Sugar, powdered: 1 cup = 130 grams
Sugar, granulated: 1 cup = 200 grams

✳ BULK INGREDIENTS ✳

Cheese: 1 lb. = 4 to 5 cups (packed), grated
Nut butter (peanut, almond, etc. — or tahini): 1 cup = 250 grams
Nuts, chopped: ⅓ to ½ cup (2 oz.) = 50 grams
Onion: 1 small to medium-sized = approximately 1 cup, chopped
Raisins: ⅓ cup (2 oz.) = 50 grams
Sesame or sunflower seeds : ¾ cup = 100 grams

[1 lb. = 454 grams]

✳ LIQUIDS ✳

1 cup (8 oz.) = 250 ml.
1 Tbs. (½ fluid oz.) = 16 ml.
16 Tbs. = 1 cup

SOUPS

A NOTE ON STOCK:

I used water instead of stock in testing these recipes. But you can make your own stock and use it wherever water is indicated. Just be sure the stock is mildly flavored, so it won't dominate the soup.

To prepare a good, mild stock, add a variety of vegetables (or their parts) to a kettleful of boiling water, and simmer, partially covered, for about an hour. Let it cool, strain it, and give it a taste test before using, to be sure it's compatible with your intended soup.

Recommended for stock:

ONIONS	ZUCCHINI	MUSHROOMS	GREEN BEANS
GARLIC	POTATOES	APPLES	LETTUCE
CARROTS	SWEET POTATOES	TOMATOES	CORN
PARSNIPS	WINTER SQUASH		

CONTENTS: SOUPS

Cream of Asparagus

The original version called for 6 Tbs. butter. This new one has just 1½ Tbs.

Preparation time: 1 hour

Yield: 4 to 5 servings

2 lbs. fresh asparagus
1½ Tbs. butter
2 cups chopped onion
1½ tsp. salt
3 Tbs. flour

2 cups water
2 cups hot milk (lowfat ok)
2 tsp. dill
½ tsp. tarragon
white pepper, to taste

1) Break off and discard the tough asparagus bottoms. Slice off the tips and set them aside. Chop the remaining stalks into 1-inch pieces.

2) Melt the butter in a medium-sized skillet. Add onion, asparagus stalks, and salt. Sauté for about 10 minutes over medium heat. When the onions are clear and soft, sprinkle in 2 Tbs. flour, while constantly stirring. Continue to cook over the lowest possible heat, stirring frequently, another 5 to 8 minutes.

3) Add water, stirring constantly. Heat to a boil, then turn down to a simmer. After about 5 minutes, sprinkle in the remaining 1 Tbs. flour, mixing well. Cook another 8 to 10 minutes, stirring frequently.

4) Purée the soup with the milk, bit by bit, in a food processor or blender. Return the purée to a kettle or large saucepan, and season with dill, tarragon, and white pepper.

5) Cut the reserved asparagus tips into small pieces, and steam until just tender. Add these to the soup, heat very gently (don't cook or boil!), and serve immediately.

Spicy Tomato Soup

Preparation time:
  50 minutes

Yield:
4 to 6
servings

1 Tbs. olive oil
1 Tbs. butter (optional)
1½ cups minced onion
3 to 4 cloves garlic, minced or crushed
½ tsp. salt
1 tsp. dill (or more, to taste)
lots of freshly ground black pepper
1 1-lb.,12-oz. can "crushed concentrated tomatoes"
2 cups water
1 Tbs. honey (optional)
1 Tbs. mayonnaise or sour cream (lowfat OK)
2 medium-sized fresh tomatoes, diced

for { yogurt
the { finely minced parsley and/or basil leaves
top { finely minced scallions or chives

1) Heat olive oil (plus or minus optional butter) in a kettle or a Dutch oven. Add onion, garlic, salt, dill, and black pepper. Stir over medium heat for about 5 to 8 minutes, or until the onions are translucent.

2) Add canned crushed tomatoes, water, and optional honey. Cover and simmer over low heat for 20 to 30 minutes.

3) About 5 minutes before serving, whisk in mayonnaise or sour cream, and stir in diced fresh tomatoes. Serve hot, topped with yogurt and freshly minced herbs.

Gypsy Soup

About 45 minutes
to prepare

NOTE: Chick peas need
to be cooked in advance. (canned = OK)

...a delicately spiced
Spanish-style
vegetable soup...

Yield: 4 to 5 servings

The vegetables in this soup can be varied. Any orange vegetable can be combined with any green. For example, peas or green beans could replace— or augment— the peppers. Carrots, pumpkin, or squash could fill in for the sweet potatoes. Innovate!

2 medium-sized ripe tomatoes	1 tsp. turmeric
2 Tbs. olive oil	1 tsp. basil
2 cups chopped onion	a dash of cinnamon
3 medium cloves garlic, crushed	a dash of cayenne
1 stalk celery, minced	1 bay leaf
2 cups peeled, diced sweet potato	3 cups water
1 tsp. salt	1 medium bell pepper, diced
2 tsp. mild paprika	1½ cups cooked chick peas

1) Heat a medium-sized saucepanful of water to boiling. Core the tomatoes, and plunge them into the boiling water for a slow count of 10. Remove the tomatoes, and peel them over a sink. Cut them open; squeeze out and discard the seeds. Chop the remaining pulp and set aside.

2) Heat the olive oil in a kettle or Dutch oven. Add onion, garlic, celery, and sweet potato, and sauté over medium heat for about 5 minutes. Add salt, and sauté 5 minutes more. Add seasonings and water, cover, and simmer about 15 minutes.

3) Add tomato pulp, bell pepper, and chick peas. Cover and simmer for about 10 more minutes, or until all the vegetables are as tender as you like them. Taste to adjust seasonings, and serve.

Light Cream of Celery Soup

2 average person's fist-sized potatoes, peeled and diced
4 cups chopped celery (in 1-inch chunks) (you'll also need
     another cup a few ingredients from now)
3 cups water
1¼ tsp. salt (plus another ½ tsp. later)
1 to 2 Tbs. butter
a heaping cup finely minced onion
a heaping cup very finely minced celery (the innermost
     stalks work best for this)
1 tsp. celery seed
1 cup milk (can be lowfat), warmed
white pepper, to taste
4 to 5 Tbs. sour cream, half and half, or heavy cream
     (optional, for a richer tasting soup)
freshly minced chives and/or parsley for garnish (some-
     thing green to liven up the appearance)

1) Place potatoes, 4 cups of celery, water, and 1¼ tsp. salt in a
medium-sized saucepan. Bring to a boil, turn the heat way down,
and simmer, covered, for about 15 minutes ~ until everything is
soft. Purée, and transfer to a larger saucepan or a kettle.

2) Melt butter in a small skillet. Add onion, finely minced celery,
celery seed, plus ½ tsp. salt. Sauté about 8 to 10 minutes ~ until
the vegetables are just tender. Add to purée.

3) Stir in remaining ingredients, except garnish. Heat gently (don't
cook or boil), and serve topped with something minced and green.

About 1 hour to prepare.
(Beans must be cooked ahead.)

Minestrone

Yield:
6 to 8
servings

For a minestrone that is more a stew than a soup, use the larger amounts of beans and pasta.

NOTE: These instructions assume the beans or chick peas are already cooked. You can soak and cook your own, or use canned (well rinsed and well drained).

2 Tbs. olive oil
2 cups chopped onion
5 medium cloves garlic, minced
1½ to 2 tsp. salt
1 stalk celery, minced
1 medium carrot, diced
1 small zucchini, diced and/or
   1 cup diced eggplant
1 tsp. oregano
fresh black pepper, to taste
1 tsp. basil

1 medium bell pepper, diced
3 to 4 cups (or more) water
1 14½-oz. can tomato purée
   (approximately 2 cups)
1 to 1½ cups cooked pea beans,
   chick peas, or kidney beans
½ to 1 cup dry pasta (any shape)
1 or 2 medium-sized ripe tomatoes,
   diced (optional)
½ cup freshly minced parsley
parmesan cheese

1) Heat the olive oil in a kettle or Dutch oven. Add onion, garlic, and 1½ tsp. salt. Sauté over medium heat for about 5 minutes, then add celery, carrot, eggplant (if using zucchini, add it later, with the bell pepper), oregano, black pepper, and basil. Cover and cook over very low heat about 10 more minutes, stirring occasionally.

2) Add bell pepper, zucchini, water, and tomato purée. Cover and simmer about 15 minutes. Add beans and simmer another 5 minutes.

3) Bring the soup to a gentle boil. Add pasta, stir, and cook until the pasta is tender. Stir in the diced fresh tomatoes, and serve right away, topped with parsley and parmesan.

Hot & Sour Soup

Preparation time:
about 45 minutes

Yield:
6 to 8
servings

1 oz. dried Chinese black mushrooms
8 cups water
3 Tbs. dry sherry or Chinese rice wine
¼ to ⅓ cup cider vinegar (to taste)
2 Tbs. soy sauce
1¾ tsp. salt
1 cake (¼ lb.) firm tofu, in thin strips
2 Tbs. cornstarch
2 beaten eggs (yolks may be omitted)
6 minced scallions (whites and greens)
¼ tsp. white pepper (to taste)
Chinese sesame oil (optional)

1) Place the dried mushrooms in a small bowl. Heat 2 (of the 8) cups of water to boiling; pour over the mushrooms. Cover with a plate, and let stand at least 30 minutes. (You can assemble the other ingredients in the meantime.) Drain the mushrooms, squeezing out and saving all the liquid. Slice the mushrooms, removing and discarding the stems.

2) In a kettle or Dutch oven, combine the remaining 6 cups of water, the reserved mushroom-soaking liquid, and the sliced mushrooms. Heat to a gentle boil.

3) Add sherry, vinegar, soy sauce, salt, and tofu. Lower the heat, and let simmer uncovered for about 10 minutes.

4) Place the cornstarch in a small bowl. Measure out about ¾ cup of the hot soup, and whisk it into the cornstarch. When the cornstarch is dissolved, stir this mixture back into the soup.

5) Drizzle the beaten eggs into the simmering soup, stirring constantly. Add scallions and white pepper. Cook only a few minutes more. Top each serving with a few drops of sesame oil, if desired.

MISO SOUP

~ almost instant soup! You can make an individual serving for your-self whenever the inspiration hits. Or you can multiply the amounts (simple math), do Step 1 in advance, and divide it into serving bowls, adding Step 2 just before serving.

Miso is a deep-flavored paste made from fermented soybeans and grains. There are several kinds available in the United States — usually in Japanese markets or in natural foods stores. The most common are red, white, Hatcho, and barley miso. Any one of them can be used to make this very simple and satisfying soup.

In traditional Japanese cooking, fish or vegetable stock (made from various kinds of seaweed) would be used to make Miso Soup. Water will also work very well, so you needn't do the extra work of making stock. But if you happen to have some good vegetable broth on hand, by all means use it.

NOTE: The optional wakame seaweed is available in Japanese markets and in some natural foods stores.

PER SERVING (easily multiplied):

1 Tbs. (more or less) miso
1 cup (more or less) boiling water
a few tiny cubes of soft tofu
a few delicate slices of scallion greens
optional additions:
• 1 to 2 Tbs. dried wakame seaweed, soaked in water for 10 to 15 minutes, then drained
• tiny carrot sticks (matchstick-like), lightly steamed
• finely shredded cabbage, lightly steamed
• a few leaves of spinach

1) Place the miso in the serving bowl. Add about ¼ cup of the boiling water and stir to make a uniform paste.

2) Stir in remaining water plus all remaining ingredients. Serve immediately.

❁ Summer Vegetable Soup ❁

Ultralight, this features the best offerings from a summer garden; it's like a salad in soup form. Use the freshest vegetables available, and make substitutions wherever necessary.

2 medium potatoes, peeled or not,
   and diced
4 cups water
3 to 4 large cloves garlic
1 to 1½ tsp. salt
black pepper, to taste
½ lb. green beans, trimmed & cut
1 cup small broccoli florets
1 cup chopped cauliflower

1 medium carrot, diced
½ lb. sugar snap or snow peas
2 small zucchini or yellow squash, diced
1 medium red bell pepper, in strips

OPTIONAL:
{
1 cup fresh corn
a small bunch spinach, chopped
1 cup buttermilk, room temperature
freshly minced herbs, for the top
}

1) Place potatoes and water in a medium-sized saucepan. Bring to a boil, lower heat, and simmer until the potatoes are tender. Add the garlic (whole cloves, peeled) during the last few minutes of simmering.

2) Purée the potatoes and garlic in their cooking water. Add salt and pepper to taste. Set aside until just before serving time.

3) Meanwhile, steam the vegetables until just tender in the following groupings: ⓐ green beans ⓑ broccoli, cauliflower, carrot ⓒ peas, zucchini, bell pepper, corn, spinach. (NOTE: A microwave does a good, fast job of steaming, with no added water.) Set the vegetables aside.

4) Heat the potato purée shortly before serving. Stir in the steamed vegetables and optional buttermilk at the last minute. Optional: a light sprinkling of freshly snipped herbs (ideally: basil, dill, parsley, and/or chives).

Succotash Chowder

Preparation time:
30 minutes, at most,
after beans are cooked

Yield: 6 servings,
possibly more

PRELIMINARY: Soak 1 to 1½ cups dry baby lima beans in water for at least 4 hours. Cook in plenty of simmering — NOT rapidly boiling — water for 35 to 40 minutes, or until perfectly tender. Try not to overcook the beans, or the soup will become gluey and lose its textural charm.

    1 medium potato (average fist-sized), diced (peeling = optional)
    1 Tbs. butter
    2 cups chopped onion
    3 to 4 medium cloves garlic, crushed or minced
    3 stalks celery, minced
    1½ tsp. salt
    1 tsp. basil
    ½ tsp. thyme
    3 cups corn (fresh OR a 1-lb. bag frozen, defrosted)
    2 to 3 cups cooked baby lima beans
    4 cups milk (can be lowfat)
    a generous amount of fresh black pepper
    finely minced parsley and/or chives (optional)

1) Cook the diced potato in boiling water until just tender. Drain well, and set aside.

2) Meanwhile, melt the butter in a kettle or Dutch oven. Add onion, garlic, celery, salt, and herbs. Sauté over medium heat for about 10 minutes, or until the onion and celery are tender. Stir in the corn, and sauté for about 10 minutes more. Add the cooked beans.

3) OPTIONAL: Purée some of the sauté in a food processor or blender. Return to the kettle. (This will make a thicker soup.)

4) Add potatoes and milk. Season to taste with black pepper; correct salt. Serve very hot, topped with minced fresh herbs, if available.

VEGETABLE CHOWDER

Instead of ¼ cup butter and ½ pint heavy cream, as in the original version, this new light one has only 1 Tbs. butter, no cream, and the option of lowfat milk. It still tastes luxurious.

Try not to shy away from the full amount of garlic. It gives the soup a rich flavor and is surprisingly smooth and subtle.

1 Tbs. butter	1 medium potato, diced
2 cups chopped onion	2 medium stalks celery, diced
6 cloves garlic, minced	2 medium carrots, diced
2 tsp. salt	2 cups chopped broccoli
½ tsp. thyme	2 cups chopped cauliflower
2 tsp. basil	½ lb. mushrooms, chopped

2 cups corn (frozen-defrosted is fine)
lots of fresh black pepper
1½ cups water
1 quart milk (lowfat ok), heated
optional: minced fresh herbs
(chives, basil, marjoram)

1) Melt the butter in a kettle or Dutch oven. Add onion, half the garlic, salt, thyme, and basil. Sauté over medium heat 5 minutes. Add potato, celery, carrots, broccoli, and cauliflower. Sauté another 5 to 8 minutes. Add mushrooms and corn, plus lots of black pepper. Sauté another 8 to 10 minutes.

2) Add water, cover, and simmer about 15 minutes, or until everything is tender. (Make sure the potatoes are done.)

3) Stir in hot milk and remaining garlic. Remove from heat until about 10 minutes before serving time, then heat gently. Serve topped with freshly minced herbs.

Chinese Vegetable Chowder

Simple and delicious ~

The mushrooms need to soak for at least 30 to 40 minutes ahead of time, and this can be done a day or two in advance.

2 oz. dried Chinese black mushrooms	black pepper, to taste
5 cups boiling water	1 medium carrot, diced
a 1-lb. package frozen corn, defrosted	1 stalk celery, minced
1 to 1½ tsp. salt	1 8-oz. can water chestnuts,
1 to 2 Tbs. soy sauce	minced

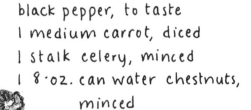

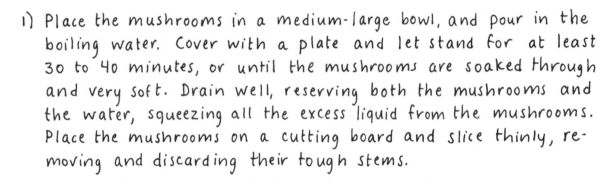

1) Place the mushrooms in a medium-large bowl, and pour in the boiling water. Cover with a plate and let stand for at least 30 to 40 minutes, or until the mushrooms are soaked through and very soft. Drain well, reserving both the mushrooms and the water, squeezing all the excess liquid from the mushrooms. Place the mushrooms on a cutting board and slice thinly, removing and discarding their tough stems.

2) Combine the mushroom water and the corn in a food processor or blender, and purée until as smooth as possible. (You will probably have to do this in more than one batch.) Transfer to a kettle or a large saucepan. (For a smoother soup, you can strain the purée on its way into the kettle.) Stir in salt, soy sauce, and black pepper to taste.

3) Lightly steam the carrot and the celery until just tender. (If you have one, a microwave oven will do this in 2 minutes.)

4) Add sliced mushrooms from Step 1, carrot, celery, and water chestnuts to the soup. Heat gently just before serving.

Cream of Broccoli

45 minutes
to prepare

Yield:
4 to 6
servings

2 Tbs. butter
1½ cups chopped onion
1 bay leaf
1 tsp. salt (more, to taste)
1 medium bell pepper, diced
4 cups chopped broccoli
2½ cups water
2 cups milk (lowfat ok)

½ cup sour cream (lowfat ok)
¼ tsp. allspice
black pepper } to taste
white pepper
a dash of thyme
½ tsp. basil
1 cup broccoli florets, sliced thin
    and lightly steamed

1) Melt butter in a kettle or Dutch oven. Add onion, bay leaf, and salt.
Sauté over medium heat until the onion is translucent.

2) Add green pepper, chopped broccoli, and water. Cover, and cook over
medium heat for 10 minutes, or until the broccoli is very tender.

3) Remove the bay leaf, and purée the soup little by little with the
milk in a blender or food processor.

4) Whisk in the sour cream and remaining seasonings. Heat gently.
Serve hot, topped with lightly steamed broccoli   florets.

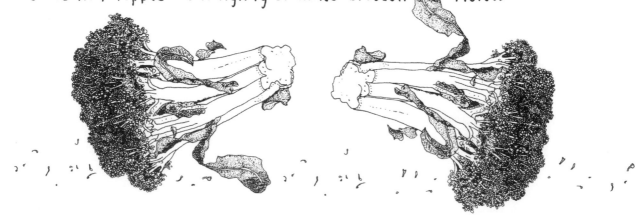

Curried Squash & Mushroom Soup

Yield: 4 or 5 servings

Preparation time: 45 minutes. (Prepare other ingredients while squash bakes.)

NOTE: This soup can be made with no dairy products.

2 medium acorn or butternut squash
2 ½ cups water
1 cup orange juice
1 Tbs. butter or oil
1 cup chopped onion
2 medium cloves garlic, crushed
1¼ tsp. salt
½ tsp. ground cumin

½ tsp. coriander
½ tsp. cinnamon
1 tsp. ginger
¼ tsp. dry mustard
½ lb. mushrooms, sliced
a few dashes cayenne (to taste)
fresh lemon juice } optional
yogurt, for the top)

1) Preheat oven to 375°F. Split the squash lengthwise, remove seeds, and place face-down on a lightly oiled tray. Bake until soft (about 30 to 40 minutes). Cool, then scoop out the insides. Measure out 3 cups'-worth, place this in a food processor or blender with the water, and purée until smooth. (You may need to do this in batches.) Transfer to a kettle, and stir in the orange juice.

2) Heat the butter or oil in a skillet, and add onion, garlic, salt, and spices. Sauté over medium heat until the onion is very soft ~ about 8 minutes.(You may need to add a small amount of water to prevent sticking.) Add mushrooms, cover, and cook about 10 minutes over medium heat, stirring occasionally.

3) Add the sauté to the squash, scraping the skillet well to salvage all the good stuff. Add cayenne and heat gently. Once it is hot, taste it to correct the seasonings. This is a fairly sweet soup; you may choose to balance this by adding fresh lemon juice to taste and/or topping each bowlful with a small spoonful of yogurt.

Cauliflower~Cheese Soup

1 medium-large potato, peeled and diced
   (about 2 to 3 cups diced)
1 large cauliflower, cut or broken into
   florets (put aside 2 cups of florets)
1 medium carrot, peeled and chopped
3 medium cloves garlic, peeled
1½ cups chopped onion
1½ tsp. salt
4 cups water
2 cups (packed) grated cheddar (plus
   extra for garnishing each serving)
3/4 cup milk (lowfat OK)
1 tsp. dill
½ tsp. caraway seeds
black pepper, to taste

1) Place potato, cauliflower (except for the 2 cups reserved), carrot, garlic, onion, salt, and water in a large saucepan. Bring to a boil, then simmer until all the vegetables are very tender. Purée in a blender or food processor, and transfer to a kettle or Dutch oven.

2) Steam the reserved cauliflower pieces until just tender. Add these to the purée along with all remaining ingredients. Heat gently, and serve topped with a little extra cheese.

◊ Split Pea Soup ◊

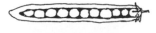

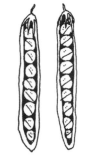

3 cups dry split peas
about 7 cups of water (more, as needed)
1 bay leaf
2 tsp. salt
½ to 1 tsp. dry mustard
2 cups minced onion
4 to 5 medium cloves garlic, crushed
3 stalks celery, minced
2 medium carrots, sliced or diced
1 small potato, thinly sliced
lots of freshly ground black pepper
3 to 4 Tbs. red wine vinegar (to taste)

TOPPINGS — Chinese sesame oil (optional)
— a fresh, ripe tomato, diced
— freshly minced parsley

1) Place split peas, water, bay leaf, salt, and dry mustard in a kettle or Dutch oven. Bring to a boil, lower heat as much as possible, and simmer, partially covered, for about 20 minutes.

2) Add onion, garlic, celery, carrots, and potato. Partially cover, and leave it to simmer gently for about 40 more minutes with occasional stirring. If necessary, add some water.

3) Add black pepper and vinegar to taste. Serve topped with a drizzle of sesame oil, diced tomato, and minced parsley.

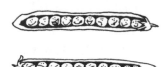

Hungarian Mushroom Soup

1 hour
to prepare

Yield:
4 to 5
servings

2 Tbs. butter
2 cups chopped onion
1½ to 2 lbs. mushrooms, sliced
1 tsp. salt
2 to 3 tsp. dried dill (or 2 to 3 Tbs. freshly minced)
1 Tbs. mild paprika
2 tsp. fresh lemon juice
3 Tbs. flour
2 cups water
1 cup milk (can be lowfat) ~ at room temperature
black pepper, to taste
½ cup sour cream
finely minced fresh parsley, for the top

1) Melt the butter in a kettle or Dutch oven. Add onions, and sauté over medium heat for about 5 minutes. Add mushrooms, salt, dill, and paprika. Stir well and cover. Let cook for about 15 more minutes, stirring occasionally. Stir in lemon juice.

2) Gradually sprinkle in the flour, stirring constantly. Cook and stir another 5 minutes or so over medium-low heat. Add water, cover, and cook about 10 minutes, stirring often.

3) Stir in milk; add black pepper to taste. Check to see if it needs more salt. Whisk in the sour cream, and heat very gently. Don't boil or cook it after this point. Serve hot, topped with freshly minced parsley.

Mushroom Bisque

2 medium potatoes (the size of an average person's fist)
1½ cups water
1 ½ Tbs. butter
2 cups chopped onion
1 small stalk celery, minced
1½ lbs. mushrooms
1½ to 2 tsp. salt
1 to 2 small cloves garlic, minced
¼ tsp. thyme
3 Tbs. dry sherry
2 tsp. soy sauce
fresh black pepper, to taste
1 cup milk (can be lowfat)
croutons (recipe on p.20)   } optional toppings
minced scallion greens or chives

1) Peel potatoes, chop into small pieces, and place in a small saucepan with the water. Cover, bring to a boil, and simmer until potatoes are tender.

2) Meanwhile, melt butter in a deep skillet or Dutch oven. Add onion and celery, and sauté over medium heat for about 5 minutes. Stir in mushrooms and salt, cover, and cook about 10 minutes, stirring occasionally. Somewhere in there, add garlic and thyme. (Adding garlic later keeps its flavor stronger.) Remove from heat; stir in sherry, soy sauce, and pepper.

3) Use a blender or food processor to purée both the potatoes in their cooking water and the mushroom sauté in its own liquid. (When you run out of the liquid, use the milk.) Combine the purées in a kettle or Dutch oven.

4) Stir, and heat gently; taste to adjust seasonings. Serve very hot, with optional but highly recommended toppings.

ONION SOUP

This soup is very, very simple and easy. Most of the preparation time, after the onions are sliced, is for simmering: slowly, thoroughly, deliciously. You can use this time to make the croutons and to prepare other components of the meal. The original recipe called for 6 Tbs. butter. I've reduced that amount to just 2 Tbs., yet the buttery flavor is still generously imparted.

2 Tbs. butter
4 large yellow onions, thinly sliced
1 tsp. salt
½ tsp. dry mustard
a dash or two of thyme
4 cups water
2 Tbs. soy sauce

2 to 3 Tbs. dry white wine (optional)
a few dashes of white pepper

TOPPINGS:
thin slices of Swiss cheese
croutons (recipe below)

1) Melt the butter in a kettle or Dutch oven. Add onions and salt, and cook over medium heat about 10 minutes, stirring occasionally.

2) Add mustard and thyme; stir and cover. Continue to cook very slowly for about 35 more minutes. The onions will be exquisitely soft and simmering in their own liquid.

3) Add water, soy sauce, optional wine, and white pepper. Simmer at least 10 minutes more. Taste to adjust seasonings. Serve topped with croutons and Swiss cheese. If you're serving the soup in ovenproof bowls, you can put them under the broiler briefly, to brown the cheese. Be careful handling the bowls!

HOMEMADE CROUTONS:

a) Sauté cubed bread in garlic butter for about 10 minutes, then transfer to a tray, and toast in a 300°F oven until crisp. OR:

b) Brush thin slices of baguette on both sides with olive oil. (Optional: crush some garlic into the oil first.) Bake on a tray in a 350°F oven until crisp (8 to 12 minutes, depending on thickness), but check on them frequently! They can look underdone one minute and burn the next.

Swiss Cheese & Onion Soup

2 Tbs. butter
2 medium onions, thinly sliced (about 4 cups)
1 to 2 medium cloves garlic, minced
1½ tsp. salt
2 tsp. dry mustard
1 to 3 Tbs. flour (depending on how thick you like your soup)
2 Tbs. dry sherry
2 cups water
1 tsp. prepared horseradish (the white kind)
1½ cups warmed milk (can be lowfat)
1½ cups (packed) grated Swiss cheese
white pepper
OPTIONAL TOPPINGS: croutons (see preceding page)
                  paprika~ or some minced pimientos

1) Melt the butter in a kettle or Dutch oven. Add onions, garlic, salt, and dry mustard, and cook over medium heat 8 to 10 minutes, or until the onions are very soft.

2) Gradually sprinkle in the flour, stirring constantly, then add the sherry and mix well. Add water and horseradish. Stir and cook for about 5 more minutes.

3) Add warm milk and cheese. After adding the cheese, stir assiduously with a wooden spoon for a good few minutes. Much to your delight, everything will become remarkably smooth and well blended.

4) Add white pepper to taste, and while you're at it, adjust the other seasonings as well. You might wish to increase the mustard, sherry, or horseradish (too late to decrease). Serve hot ~ plain, or topped with croutons and/or a light dusting of paprika and/or a small amount of finely minced pimiento.

CARROT SOUP VARIATIONS

Each of the following Carrot Soup Variations is a thick, creamy purée that can be made with no dairy products. Each soup also keeps and freezes very well, and doesn't suffer from repeated reheatings.

Gingered Carrot Soup

Serve this as a thick sauce over rice for a simple supper. It also goes well with Samosas (p.170) and Raita (p.99).

2 lbs. carrots
4 cups water
1 Tbs. butter or oil
1½ cups chopped onion
2 medium cloves garlic, minced
2 Tbs. freshly grated ginger
1½ tsp. salt

¼ tsp. each: cumin
ground fennel
cinnamon
allspice
dried mint

3 to 4 Tbs. fresh lemon juice
1 cup lightly toasted cashews
OPTIONAL: buttermilk, to
drizzle on top

1) Peel and trim carrots, and cut them into 1-inch chunks. Place in a medium-large saucepan with the water, cover, and bring to a boil. Lower the heat, and simmer until very tender (about 10 to 15 minutes, depending on the size of the carrot pieces).

2) Meanwhile heat the butter or oil in a small skillet. Add onions, and sauté over medium heat for about 5 minutes. Add garlic, ginger, salt, and spices. Turn heat to low, and continue to sauté for another 8 to 10 minutes, or until everything is well mingled and the onions are very soft. Stir in lemon juice.

3) Use a food processor or blender to purée everything together (including the toasted cashews). You will need to do this in several batches. Transfer the purée to a kettle, and heat gently just before serving. If desired, pass a small pitcher of buttermilk, for individual drizzlings.

Herbed Carrot Soup

2 lbs. carrots
1 medium potato (the size of a medium fist)
4 cups water
1 Tbs. butter or oil
1 cup chopped onion
1 ½ tsp. salt
2 medium cloves garlic, minced or crushed
½ tsp. thyme
½ tsp. marjoram or oregano
1 tsp. basil
1 to 2 Tbs. lemon juice (or, to taste)
optional: small amounts of finely minced
             fresh mint,
                chives,
                and or
                parsley,
             for the top

1) Peel and chop the carrots and potato, and place them in a medium-large saucepan with the water. Bring to a boil, cover, and simmer until the vegetables are tender (10 to 15 minutes).

2) Meanwhile, heat oil in a small skillet. Add onions and salt, and sauté over medium heat for about 5 minutes. Add garlic and dried herbs, and sauté about 5 minutes more, or until the onions are soft. Stir in lemon juice.

3) Purée everything together in a blender or food processor, and transfer to a kettle or Dutch oven. Simmer gently 8 to 10 minutes. Serve hot, topped with a light sprinkling of fresh herbs.

White Bean & Black Olive Soup

NOTE: This recipe calls for 2 cups cooked white pea beans. Use 1 cup dry, and cook them, without prior soaking, in plenty of simmering (<u>not</u> rapidly boiling) water until tender (about 1¼ hours).

2 Tbs. olive oil
1 heaping cup chopped onion
1 stalk celery, diced
1 medium carrot, diced
1 to 1½ tsp. salt
1 tsp. oregano or marjoram
1½ tsp. basil
1 small (5 to 6 inches long) zucchini, diced
1 small bell pepper, chopped
3 to 4 medium cloves garlic, crushed
fresh black pepper
4 cups water
3 oz. (half a small can) tomato paste
¼ cup dry red wine (optional)
2 cups cooked white pea beans
1 cup sliced Kalamata (Greek) olives (or plain black ones)
1 Tbs. fresh lemon juice
finely minced fresh parsley ⎫
a ripe tomato, diced   ⎬ TOPPINGS

1) Heat the olive oil in a kettle or Dutch oven. Add onion, celery, carrot, salt, and herbs. Sauté over medium heat 8 to 10 minutes, or until the vegetables are just tender.

2) Add zucchini, bell pepper, and garlic. Sauté 5 minutes more. Grind in some black pepper.

3) Combine water and tomato paste. Add to vegetables, along with the remaining ingredients, except toppings. Cover and simmer over low heat for about 15 minutes. Serve hot, topped with parsley and diced tomato.

Lentil Soup

...... gentle.

This lentil soup just about cooks itself.
Only one pot is needed, so cleanup is easy.

3 cups dry lentils
7 cups water
2 tsp. salt
6 to 8 medium cloves garlic, crushed
2 cups chopped onion
2 stalks celery, chopped
2 medium carrots, sliced or diced
Optional: ½ to 1 tsp. basil
          ½ tsp. thyme
          ½ tsp. oregano
lots of freshly ground black pepper
2 to 3 medium-sized ripe tomatoes
red wine vinegar } to drizzle on top
olive oil

Preparation
time:
about 1 hour

Yield:
6 to 8
servings

1) Place lentils, water, and salt in a kettle. Bring to a boil, lower heat to the slowest possible simmer, and cook quietly, partially covered, for 20 to 30 minutes.

2) Add vegetables (except tomatoes), herbs, and black pepper. Partially cover, and let simmer peacefully another 20 to 30 minutes, stirring occasionally.

3) Heat a medium saucepanful of water to boiling. Drop in the tomatoes for 10 seconds, then take them out, peel off the skins, and squeeze out the seeds. Chop the remaining pulp and add to the soup. Let the soup cook for at least 5 minutes more.

4) Serve hot, with a drizzle of vinegar and olive oil on top.

Brazilian Black Bean Soup

About 1¼ hours
to prepare.
(Get everything
else done while
the beans cook.)

PRELIMINARY: Soak 2 cups dry black beans in plenty
of water for at least 4 hours (and preferably
overnight.)

2 cups dry black beans, soaked
4 cups water
1 Tbs. olive oil
3 cups chopped onion
10 medium cloves garlic, crushed
2 tsp. cumin
2 to 2½ tsp. salt
1 medium carrot, diced

1 medium bell pepper, diced
1½ cups orange juice
black pepper, to taste
cayenne, to taste
2 medium tomatoes, diced (optional)

optional toppings: { sour cream
cilantro
salsa (recipe p. 96)

1) Place the soaked beans in a kettle or Dutch oven with 4 cups water.
Bring to a boil, cover, and simmer until tender (about 1¼ hours).

2) Heat olive oil in a medium-sized skillet. Add onion, half the garlic,
cumin, salt, and carrot. Sauté over medium heat until the carrot is
just tender. Add remaining garlic and the bell pepper. Sauté until everything is very tender (another 10 to 15 minutes). Add the sautéed
mixture to the beans, scraping in every last morsel.

3) Stir in orange juice, black pepper, cayenne, and optional tomatoes.
Purée all or some of the soup in a blender or food processor, and
return to kettle. Simmer over very low heat 10 to 15 minutes more.
Serve topped with an artful arrangement of sour cream, cilantro,
and salsa.

RUSSIAN CABBAGE BORSCHT

Preparation time: 1 hour

Yield: 4 to 6 servings

1½ cups thinly sliced potato
1 cup thinly sliced beets
4 cups water
1 to 2 Tbs. butter
1½ cups chopped onion
1 scant tsp. caraway seeds
1½ tsp. salt (or more, to taste)

1 stalk celery, chopped
1 medium-sized carrot, sliced
3 to 4 cups shredded cabbage
freshly ground black pepper
1 tsp. dill (plus extra, for garnish)
1 to 2 Tbs. cider vinegar
1 to 2 Tbs. brown sugar or honey
1 cup tomato purée

TOPPINGS { sour cream or yogurt
{ extra dill

1) Place potatoes, beets, and water in a medium-sized saucepan.
Cover, and cook over medium heat until tender (20 to 30 minutes).

2) Meanwhile, melt the butter in a kettle or Dutch oven. Add onion,
caraway seeds, and salt. Cook over medium heat, stirring occasionally, until the onions are translucent (8 to 10 minutes).

3) Add celery, carrots, and cabbage, plus 2 cups of the cooking
water from the potatoes and beets. Cover and cook over medium
heat until the vegetables are tender (another 8 to 10 minutes).

4) Add the remaining ingredients (including all the potato and beet
water), cover, and simmer for at least 15 more minutes. Taste to
correct seasonings, and serve hot, topped with sour cream or
yogurt and a light dusting of dill.

Mushroom-Barley Soup

Preparation time: 1¼ hours

Yield: 6 to 8 servings

½ cup uncooked pearl barley
6½ cups water
1 to 2 Tbs. butter
1 medium onion, chopped (about 1½ cups)
2 medium cloves garlic, minced
1 lb. mushrooms, sliced
½ to 1 tsp. salt
3 to 4 Tbs. soy sauce
3 to 4 Tbs. dry sherry
freshly ground black pepper

1) Place the barley and 1½ cups of the water in a large saucepan or a Dutch oven. Bring to a boil, cover, and simmer until the barley is tender (20 to 30 minutes).

2) Meanwhile, melt the butter in a skillet. Add the onions and sauté for about 5 minutes over medium heat. Add garlic, mushrooms, and ½ tsp. salt. Cover and cook, stirring occasionally, until everything is very tender ~ about 10 to 12 minutes. Stir in soy sauce and sherry.

3) Add the sauté with all its liquid to the cooked barley, along with the remaining 5 cups of water. Grind in a generous amount of black pepper, and simmer, partially covered, another 20 minutes over very low heat. Taste to correct seasonings, and serve.

POTATO·FENNEL SOUP
~with Browned Onions~

Preparation time:
about 40 minutes

Yield:
about 6 servings

This very simple and rich-tasting soup can be made with no dairy products.

Fennel is well known as a seasoning, particularly in seed form. It is less well known as a vegetable: a light green bulb that is crunchy, juicy, and deeply, though subtly, flavored.

1 Tbs. butter or oil
4 cups thinly sliced onions
2 tsp. salt
4 medium potatoes (average fist-size), not necessarily peeled, and sliced into thin pieces 1 to 2 inches long
1 cup freshly minced fennel bulb
½ tsp. caraway seeds
4 cups water
white pepper, to taste
OPTIONAL TOPPINGS:
   ~ Sour cream, thinned (by beating with a little whisk in a little bowl)
   ~ the feathery tops of the fennel, well minced

1) Melt the butter (or heat the oil) in a kettle or Dutch oven. Add the onions and 1 tsp. salt. Cook over medium-low heat, stirring occasionally, for about 15 to 20 minutes, or until the onions are very, very soft and lightly browned.

2) Add the potatoes, another ½ tsp. salt, the minced fennel bulb, and the caraway seeds. Sauté over medium heat for another 5 minutes, then add the water. Bring to a boil, then partially cover, and simmer until the potatoes are tender (10 to 15 minutes).

3) Taste to adjust salt; add white pepper. Serve hot, topped with a decorative swirl of thinned sour cream and/or minced feathery fennel tops.

Cream of Spinach Soup

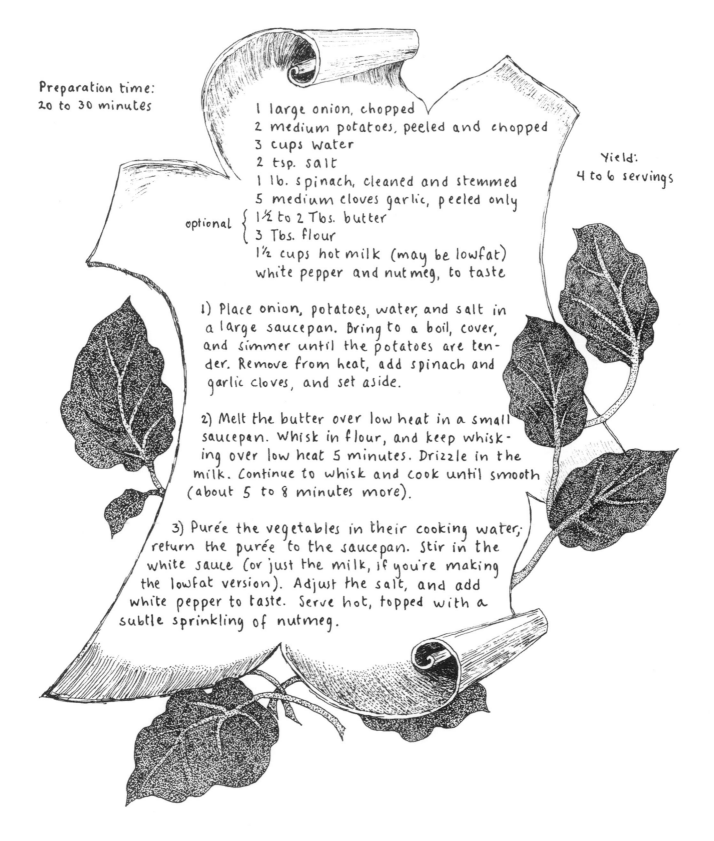

1 large onion, chopped
2 medium potatoes, peeled and chopped
3 cups water
2 tsp. salt
1 lb. spinach, cleaned and stemmed
5 medium cloves garlic, peeled only
optional { 1½ to 2 Tbs. butter
{ 3 Tbs. flour
1½ cups hot milk (may be lowfat)
white pepper and nutmeg, to taste

1) Place onion, potatoes, water, and salt in a large saucepan. Bring to a boil, cover, and simmer until the potatoes are tender. Remove from heat, add spinach and garlic cloves, and set aside.

2) Melt the butter over low heat in a small saucepan. Whisk in flour, and keep whisking over low heat 5 minutes. Drizzle in the milk. Continue to whisk and cook until smooth (about 5 to 8 minutes more).

3) Purée the vegetables in their cooking water; return the purée to the saucepan. Stir in the white sauce (or just the milk, if you're making the lowfat version). Adjust the salt, and add white pepper to taste. Serve hot, topped with a subtle sprinkling of nutmeg.

Gazpacho

20 to 30 minutes
to prepare,
plus time to chill.

Yield:
6 servings

4 cups tomato juice

½ cup finely minced onion

1 medium clove garlic, minced

1 medium bell pepper, minced

1 tsp. honey (optional)

1 medium cucumber,
peeled, seeded, & minced

2 scallions, minced

juice of ½ lemon + 1 lime

2 Tbs. wine vinegar

1 tsp. each <tarragon basil

¼ to ½ tsp. cumin

¼ cup freshly minced parsley

2 to 3 Tbs. olive oil

salt, black pepper, and
cayenne — to taste

2 cups freshly diced tomatoes

Combine all ingredients.

(Optional: purée all or some)

Chill until very cold.

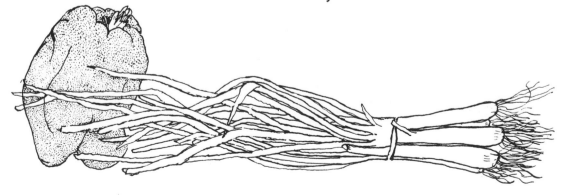

Chilled Cucumber-Yogurt Soup

Preparation time:
less than 10 minutes,
plus time to chill.

4 cups peeled, seeded, &
  grated cucumber
2 cups water
2 cups yogurt (nonfat OK)
½ to 1 tsp. salt
1 small clove garlic, minced
1 tsp. dried dill (or 1 Tbs. fresh)
1 Tbs. honey (optional)
minced fresh mint and chives

Yield:
4 to 6
servings

Combine grated cucumber, water, yogurt, salt, garlic, dill, and optional honey in a medium-sized bowl. Stir until well blended, and chill until very cold. Serve topped with finely minced fresh herbs, if available.

~chilled, creamy
potato-onion soup

Vichyssoise

Preparation time:
   45 minutes,
plus time to chill

Yield:
about 6 servings

2 Tbs. butter
3 cups chopped onions
1 to 1½ tsp. salt
4 medium potatoes (about 2 lbs.),
   peeled and diced
4 cups water

2 cups milk (lowfat ok)
OPTIONAL: up to ½ pint heavy cream
white pepper, to taste
freshly minced chives for the top

1) Melt the butter in a kettle or Dutch oven. Add onions and salt, and sauté about 15 minutes, or until the onions are very soft and beginning to brown.

2) Add potatoes and water, and bring to a boil. Lower heat, cover, and simmer until the potatoes are tender (about 10 to 15 minutes).

3) Purée until very smooth in a blender or food processor, and transfer to a medium-large container. Stir in the milk and optional cream; add white pepper.

4) Chill until very cold. Serve topped with finely minced fresh chives.

Green
Variation

Make Vichyssoise exactly as described above. When stirring in the milk, also add some combination (the more, the better) of puréed:

   steamed spinach,
      steamed zucchini,
         steamed Boston (a.k.a. "butter") lettuce
            fresh watercress
               fresh herbs (basil, dill, parsley)
Top each serving with:

   peeled, seeded, and coarsely grated cucumber.

Cascadilla

Preparation time:
15 minutes,
plus time to chill

Yield:
4 to 6
servings

1 small cucumber~ peeled,
   seeded, and minced
1 scallion, finely minced
1 small clove garlic, crushed
½ tsp. dill
4 cups tomato juice

1 cup yogurt (nonfat OK)
1 small bell pepper, minced
3 to 4 raw mushrooms,
   thinly sliced
salt and pepper, to taste
OPTIONAL { croutons (p.20)
{ minced watercress

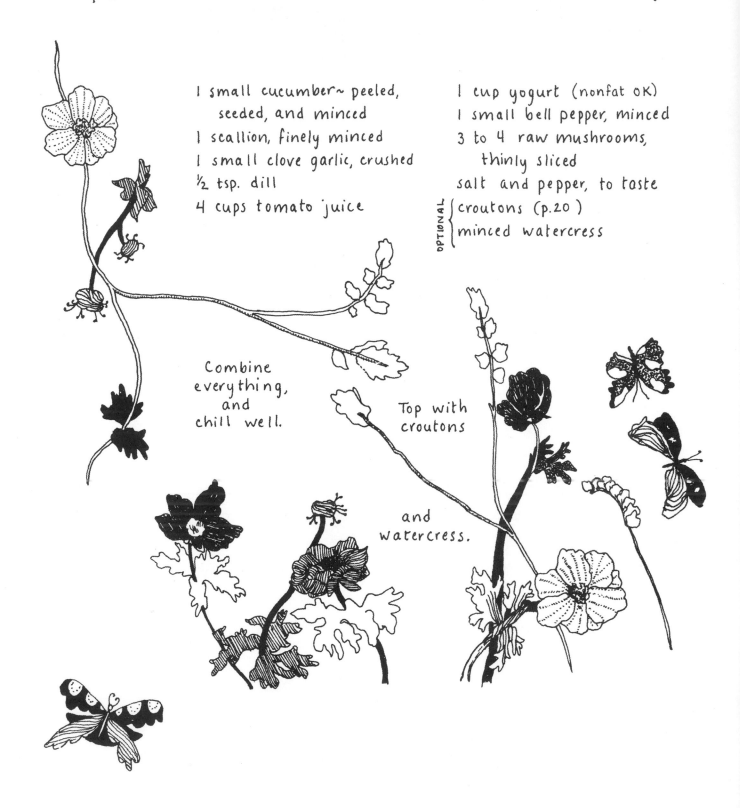

Combine
everything,
and
chill well.

Top with
croutons

and
watercress.

Chilled Beet Borscht

Preparation time:
about 40 minutes,
plus time to chill.

Yield: about
6 servings

4 large (3-inch diameter) beets
3 cups water
1 tsp. salt
1 to 2 Tbs. lemon juice, to taste
2 to 3 Tbs. sugar or honey, to taste
black pepper
1 to 2 Tbs. freshly minced dill (or 2 tsp. dried)
1 medium cucumber, peeled, seeded, and grated
2 to 3 finely minced scallions (whites and greens)
OPTIONAL: 1 medium-sized dill pickle, finely minced
2 cups buttermilk

OPTIONAL GARNISHES
{ a spoonful of sour cream or yogurt (nonfat OK)
slices of boiled potato
chopped hardboiled egg

1) Peel and trim the beets, and place them in a medium-sized saucepan with the water and salt. Bring to a boil, lower heat, partially cover, and simmer until the beets are tender (about 20 to 30 minutes). Remove the beets with a slotted spoon, and transfer the water to a medium-large bowl or container.

2) When the beets are cool enough to handle, grate them coarsely and return them to the water. Stir in remaining ingredients, except buttermilk and garnishes. Cover and chill until cold.

3) When the borscht is cold, stir in the buttermilk. Taste to adjust salt, pepper, lemon juice, sugar or honey. Serve topped with any combination of garnishes.

Chilled Berry Soup

Much more than just a soup, this refreshing tart-sweet preparation can be a summer beverage, a breakfast dish, or even a dessert.

Frozen berries work very well in here, so you don't need to wait for perfect fresh ones. Blue-, black-, rasp-, and strawberries can all be found in frozen, unsweetened form in the supermarket. You can also freeze your own during an abundant season. Frozen berries give off generous amounts of pure berry juice as they defrost, and you can include all of it in the soup. It creates an indescribably lovely color.

3 cups orange juice (preferably fresh-squeezed)
3 cups buttermilk or yogurt (nonfat OK)
1 to 2 Tbs. fresh lemon or lime juice
optional: 1 to 2 Tbs. sugar or honey
2 to 3 cups berries ~ any kind or any combination
    (Leave smaller berries whole. Larger ones
        should be sliced.)
optional: ⌐ a dash of cinnamon and/or nutmeg
          a few sprigs of fresh mint, for garnish

1) Whisk together orange juice and buttermilk or yogurt. Add lemon or lime juice and optional sugar or honey (or not), to taste. Cover and chill until serving time.

2) When you're ready to serve, place about ½ cup berries in each bowl. Ladle the soup on top. If desired, dust very lightly with cinnamon and/or nutmeg, and garnish with a few small sprigs of mint.

SALADS

CONTENTS: SALADS

a good method for assembling
🍃 GREEN LEAFY SALADS 🍃

Assembling a green salad is a highly personalized endeavor, and of course there is no absolutely correct method. But the truth is, some salads are much better than others. Here are a few guidelines to help your salads be among the better ones:

🍃 1) Use a large enough bowl, so you'll have plenty of room to toss the salad thoroughly. Make it your special salad bowl — it will acquire more depth and soul with each use, and this will enhance something nameless (I don't know what) about the experience.

🍃 2) The basis for a green leafy salad is leafy greens: lettuces, spinach, and other tender green leaves that can be eaten raw. Use only the freshest greens! They should be immaculate and absolutely dry (use a salad spinner plus paper towels). Store in a crisper or in dry plastic bags in the refrigerator.

🍃 3) The optional extras = delicate clippings, shavings, and gratings of other vegetables, plus cherry or plum tomatoes, olives, nuts, slices of fruit (anything from apple or pear slices to citrus sections to fresh figs), crumbled pungent cheese, grated hardboiled egg, or homemade croutons (see p. 20). Have whatever you choose to add ready to be mixed in gently or laid on top just before serving.

🍃 4) If you want to make the dressing right in the bowl as you toss the salad, place a few tablespoons of olive oil, nut oil, or a combination in the bottom of the bowl with a clove or two of crushed garlic. Add crisp, dry greens a handful at a time, and toss after each addition, making sure everything gets evenly coated. Add small amounts of additional oil, if needed, plus small amounts of salt and vinegar (red wine, herb-infused, balsamic, fruit-flavored — experiment!) right before serving, and add optional extras. Bring a pepper mill to the table.

RULE OF THUMB: Be a benefactor with the oil,
a miser with the vinegar,
a poet with the salt, and
a demon with the pepper!

Warm Salad

... featuring an assortment of ultranutritious leafy greens, lightly cooked and delicately marinated. This can be a main dish unto itself, or a prelude or accompaniment to a simple pasta supper. However you serve it, be sure to include some fresh crusty bread to mop up the juices.

NOTE: Other types of greens can be substituted for the escarole, chard, and mustard. Try kale, collard, or dandelion greens.

3 Tbs. olive oil
1 small bunch escarole, chopped
1 medium bunch red or green chard, chopped
about 8 large leaves Napa or savoy cabbage, chopped
2 cups (packed) chopped mustard greens

1 to 2 tsp. salt
2 large cloves garlic, minced
2 medium leeks, chopped
2 cups chopped red onion
3/4 lb. mushrooms, sliced

1 stalk celery, sliced
1/2 small cauliflower, chopped
3 Tbs. balsamic or wine vinegar
6 Tbs. (or more) parmesan
lots of fresh black pepper

1) Heat 1 Tbs. olive oil in a large wok or deep skillet. Add the escarole, chard, cabbage, and mustard greens, a little at a time, salting lightly after each addition, and adding more greens as soon as the ones in the pot cook down enough to make room. Use a fairly intense level of heat under the pot, and stir as you cook. When all the greens are wilted and tender, stir in the garlic. Cook and stir just a minute or two more, then transfer to a platter.

2) Add the remaining oil to the wok or skillet, and when it is hot, add leeks, onion, mushrooms, celery, and cauliflower. Salt lightly, and stir-fry quickly over medium-high heat until just tender (about 5 to 8 minutes). Add to the platter, mix gently to incorporate the greens, and sprinkle with vinegar and parmesan while still hot. Grind black pepper over the top, and serve hot, warm, or at room temperature, with thick slices of toasted bread to mop up the juices. (Sourdough bread is especially good for this.)

RAW VEGETABLE SALAD
. . . .

Most vegetables can be eaten raw if cut properly. In this salad, everything is minced very small or grated, so chewing is light and delightful and not a cumbersome chore. Visually, Raw Vegetable Salad can be beautiful, like edible confetti. Serve in glass bowls to maximize the aesthetic impact.

Use whatever is in season, and in any proportion. Sprouts, tomatoes, and/or mushroom slices can be used as toppings. Try pairing this salad with the Very Green Dressing, which follows.

carrots	beets
celery	cucumber
broccoli	green beans
cauliflower	sugar snap or snow peas
cabbage (green and red)	red onion
bell peppers (all colors)	scallions
zucchini or summer squash	radishes
spinach	fresh herbs

Peel wherever necessary; mince or grate everything and mix well.

VERY GREEN DRESSING
. . . .

3-4 Tbs. olive oil
a handful of parsley
a handful of fresh spinach
½ a small zucchini, cut in chunks
10 to 15 fresh basil leaves (2 tsp. dried)
1 medium clove garlic
1 cup buttermilk
¼ to ½ tsp. salt
1 tsp. lemon juice
OPTIONAL: a few pieces of ripe avocado;
    moderate amounts of other fresh
    herbs (chives, dill, cilantro)

whip it up in a blender or food processor. Makes a generous cup.

SPECIAL SALAD DRESSINGS

BASIC VINAIGRETTE
~ the basic dressing for green salads. It keeps for weeks.

1 cup olive oil
4 to 5 Tbs. red wine vinegar
½ to 1 tsp. salt
1 to 2 medium cloves garlic, minced

} Combine everything in a jar. Cover tightly and shake well.

VINAIGRETTE VARIATIONS: (These are just a few suggestions. You can experiment even further with your own ideas.)

* add 3 to 4 Tbs. orange or apple juice, or
    2 Tbs. lemon juice plus a little grated lemon rind, plus
* very finely minced parsley and/or
* very finely minced other herbs (fresh or dried basil, dill, marjoram, chives, thyme)
* substitute some of the olive oil with a nut oil
* substitute different flavors of vinegar (fruit-infused, balsamic, champagne, etc.)
* add 1 to 2 tsp. good quality mustard
* for creamy vinaigrette: add 2 to 3 Tbs. mayonnaise, sour cream, or yogurt

SWEET & TART MUSTARD DRESSING
~ good on chilled cooked vegetables, especially Brussels sprouts, cauliflower, or broccoli

6 Tbs. olive oil
2 Tbs. Dijon mustard
4 Tbs. red wine vinegar
2 tsp. real maple syrup or honey
salt and pepper, to taste

} Whisk everything together. Cover and chill.

RANCH DRESSING

~ good on leafy salads made of sturdy greens, like romaine or spinach.

1 cup buttermilk
optional: 2 to 3 Tbs. sour cream or mayonnaise (see p.44) OR
       ¼ cup lowfat cottage cheese
2 to 3 Tbs. dried onion flakes
¼ to ½ tsp. salt (to taste)
1 tsp. lemon juice
lots of black pepper

~ whisk everything together. Keep in a tightly covered container in the refrigerator.

CREAMY ROQUEFORT DRESSING
~ Make Ranch Dressing, and add ½ cup crumbled Roquefort.

CREAMY GARLIC DRESSING
~ Make Ranch Dressing, and add 1 to 2 cloves crushed garlic.

GAZPACHO DRESSING

1 cup tomato juice
1 cup diced cucumber (peeled and seeded)
1 minced scallion
1 medium clove garlic
a few leaves fresh basil (or ½ tsp. dried)
1 to 2 Tbs. fresh (or 1 to 2 tsp. dried) dill
a small handful of fresh parsley
1 to 2 tsp. lemon or lime juice
3-4 Tbs. olive oil
salt and pepper, to taste

Purée everything together in a blender or food processor. Cover tightly and chill.

HOMEMADE MAYONNAISE:

REGULAR (REAL) MAYONNAISE:

1 large egg
3 Tbs. cider vinegar
½ tsp. salt
½ tsp. dry mustard
1¼ cups olive oil

1) Place the first 4 ingredients in a blender or food processor, along with 2 Tbs. of the oil. Process for a few seconds.

2) Keep the motor running as you drizzle in the remaining oil. As soon as all the oil is incorporated, turn off the machine. Scrape the mayonnaise into a container, cover, and refrigerate.

TOFU (SOMEWHAT REAL) MAYONNAISE:

1 packed cup mashed tofu (firm or silken)
1 small clove garlic
1 tsp. good-quality prepared mustard
2 tsp. cider vinegar
¼ to ½ tsp. salt (to taste)
¼ cup olive oil

1) Place everything except the oil in a blender or food processor. Process until very smooth.

2) Keep the machine running as you drizzle in the oil. When all the oil is incorporated, turn off the machine. Transfer to a container, cover, and refrigerate.

VARIATIONS (use with either of the above):

GREEN MAYO: Add a handful each of chopped parsley and chives to step 1.

SESAME MAYO: Substitute a few tablespoons of the oil with Chinese sesame oil.

40 minutes to prepare,
plus time to marinate.
TIME SAVER: Prepare
other things while the
eggplant cooks.

Macedonian Salad

Yield: 4 to 6 servings
(possibly more,
depending on the
context)

...small cubes of roasted eggplant, marinated with fresh vegetables
in a lemony, herby vinaigrette

1 large eggplant (about 9 inches long)-- or its approximate
equivalent in medium or small eggplants -- peeled or not,
and cut into 1-inch cubes, or even smaller

a little oil, for the baking tray

4 Tbs. olive oil	¼ cup (packed) finely minced parsley
2 Tbs. red wine vinegar	2 small scallions, very finely minced
1 medium clove garlic, minced	½ medium red bell pepper, minced
½ tsp. salt (more, to taste)	½ medium green bell pepper, minced
freshly ground black pepper	1 medium tomato, diced
½ tsp. basil	**OPTIONAL GARNISHES:**
¼ tsp. thyme	olives (Greek, oil-cured, or Niçoise)
¼ tsp. marjoram or oregano	yogurt
1 Tbs. fresh lemon juice	crumbled feta cheese

1) Preheat oven to 375°F. Spread the eggplant cubes onto a lightly oiled
baking tray, and roast in the oven about 15 minutes, or until tender
enough so a fork can slide in easily. Remove from oven.

2) Meanwhile, combine the olive oil, vinegar, garlic, salt, pepper, herbs,
and lemon juice in a medium-sized bowl. Add the still-warm eggplant
and stir. Cover, and let sit for at least 2 hours. (At this stage, it will keep
in the refrigerator for several days.)

3) Add the remaining vegetables within an hour or two of serving. Serve
garnished with olives and yogurt or crumbled feta cheese.

Tabouli

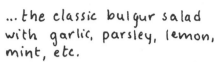

...the classic bulgur salad with garlic, parsley, lemon, mint, etc.

6-8 servings

30 to 40 minutes to prepare

You can prepare Steps 1 and 2 as much as a day or two in advance. The flavors get deeper as it sits around. A food processor does a perfect job of mincing scallions, parsley, and mint into a fine feathery state, which makes the salad much prettier and easier to eat.

1 cup dry bulgur wheat
1½ cups boiling water
1 to 1½ tsp. salt
¼ cup fresh lemon juice
¼ cup olive oil
2 medium cloves garlic, crushed
black pepper, to taste

4 scallions, finely minced (whites & greens)
1 packed cup minced parsley
10 to 15 fresh mint leaves, minced
   (or 1 to 2 Tbs. dried mint)
2 medium-sized ripe tomatoes, diced
OPTIONAL: • ½ cup cooked chick peas
   • 1 medium bell pepper, diced
   • 1 small cucumber, seeded & minced

1) Combine bulgur and boiling water in a medium-large bowl. Cover and let stand until the bulgur is tender (20 to 30 minutes, minimum).

2) Add salt, lemon juice, olive oil, garlic, and black pepper, and mix thoroughly. Cover tightly and refrigerate until about 30 minutes before serving.

3) About 30 minutes before serving, stir in remaining ingredients (including optional additions) and mix well. Serve cold with warm wedges of lightly toasted pita bread. (For more serving ideas, see Mezza, p. 100.)

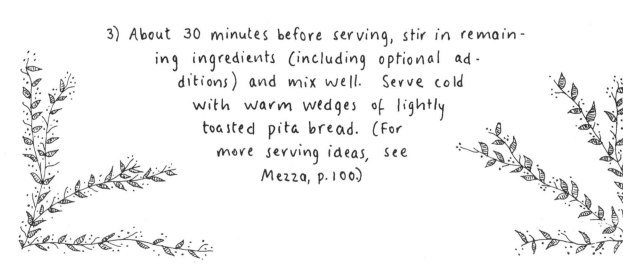

Lentil-Bulgur Salad

Similar to Tabouli, but more complex (although no more difficult to prepare), this salad is a perfectly balanced protein dish that can be served as a main course ~ especially for lunch on a hot summer day. All you need to complete the meal is toasted pita bread and some ripe fresh fruit for dessert. This is also a good dish to bring to potluck parties. You can easily double the amounts.

{ 1 cup dry lentils
{ 2 cups water

{ 1 cup dry bulgur wheat
{ 1 cup boiling water

¼ cup olive oil
¼ cup lemon juice
2 medium cloves garlic, crushed
1 tsp. salt
½ tsp. oregano
2 Tbs. freshly minced mint
   (or 2 tsp. dried mint)

2 to 3 Tbs. freshly minced dill
   (or 2 to 3 tsp. dried dill)
fresh black pepper, to taste
¼ cup (packed) freshly minced parsley
⅓ cup finely minced red onion
1 small bell pepper (any color), diced
½ stalk celery, finely minced
½ cup crumbled feta cheese
½ cup Niçoise olives (a scant ¼ lb.)
1 medium-sized tomato, diced
½ cup chopped toasted walnuts
squeezable wedges of lemon,
   for garnish

1) Place the lentils in a medium-sized saucepan, cover with water, and bring just to the boiling point. Turn the heat way down, partially cover, and allow to simmer without agitation for 20 to 25 minutes ~ or until tender but not mushy. Drain well, then transfer to a large bowl.

2) While the lentils are cooking, place the bulgur in a small bowl. Add boiling water, cover with a plate, and let stand 10 to 15 minutes while getting the other ingredients ready.

3) Add everything to the lentils, except tomato chunks, walnuts, and lemon wedges. Mix gently but thoroughly. Cover tightly and refrigerate.

4) Just before serving, top with tomatoes and walnuts. Garnish with lemon wedges.

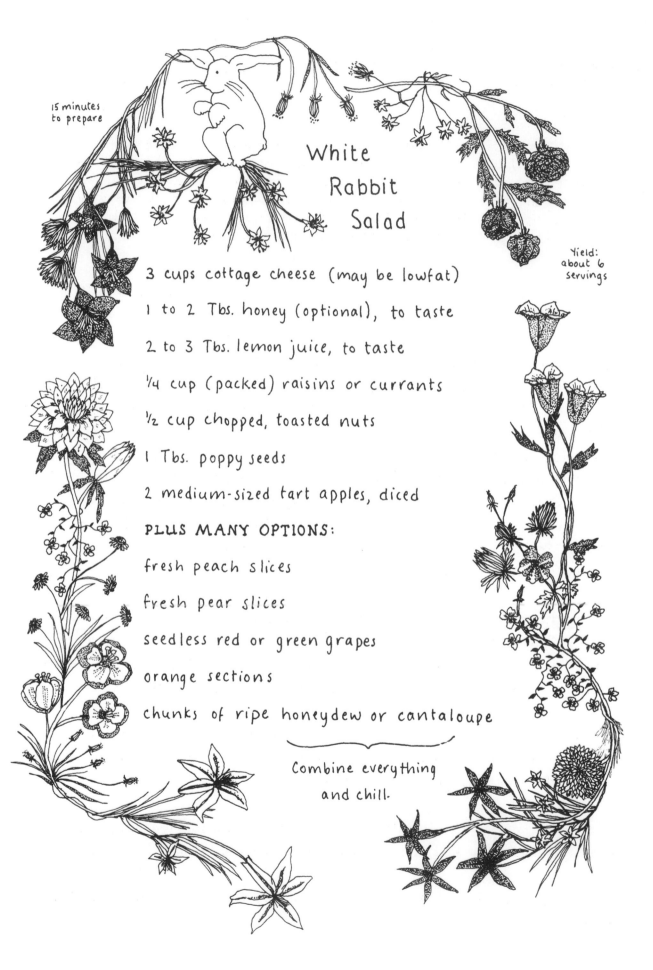

White Rabbit Salad

3 cups cottage cheese (may be lowfat)

1 to 2 Tbs. honey (optional), to taste

2 to 3 Tbs. lemon juice, to taste

¼ cup (packed) raisins or currants

½ cup chopped, toasted nuts

1 Tbs. poppy seeds

2 medium-sized tart apples, diced

PLUS MANY OPTIONS:

fresh peach slices

fresh pear slices

seedless red or green grapes

orange sections

chunks of ripe honeydew or cantaloupe

Combine everything
and chill.

March Hare

Invented in
March 1973

15 minutes
to prepare

6 to 8
servings

COMBINE AND CHILL:

3 cups cottage cheese (may be lowfat)

2 Tbs. toasted sesame seeds

1/4 cup lightly toasted sunflower seeds

1 medium carrot, diced very small

1 medium-sized ripe tomato, diced

1 scallion (whites and greens included), minced

1 small bell pepper ~ any color, minced

1 stalk celery, diced

1 small cucumber ~ peeled, seeded, and minced

1/2 cup (packed) finely minced parsley

a handful or two of alfalfa sprouts

2 to 3 Tbs. fresh lemon juice ⎫
                                 ⎬ to taste
salt (optional) & black pepper ⎭

1 to 2 hardboiled eggs, chopped (optional)

🌸 Thai Salad 🌸

Made entirely with ordinary and familiar supermarket items, this salad, with its tart-sweet-spicy-peanutty dressing, is surprisingly exotic. It's also very much fun to eat.

NOTE: Potatoes and eggs need to be cooked in advance. Ditto if you choose to fry the tofu. The dressing keeps for weeks, so make it any time.

THE DRESSING:

Place the peanut butter in a small bowl. Whisk in the water, and beat until well combined. Stir in remaining ingredients.

- 6 Tbs. good peanut butter
- 1 cup boiling water
- 4 Tbs. cider vinegar
- 1 Tbs. sugar or honey
- 1 to 1½ tsp. salt
- 3 to 4 medium cloves garlic, minced
- crushed red pepper or cayenne, to taste
- 2 tsp. lemon or lime juice

THE REST:

Pile up everything in a provocative yet compelling arrangement. Drizzle the dressing on top.

- 1 medium head crisp lettuce (Romaine is good.)
- 1 medium carrot, shredded or thinly sliced
- 1 small bell pepper, in thin strips
- 1 small cucumber ~ peeled, seeded, and sliced
- 2 medium-sized ripe tomatoes, in bite-sized chunks
- 2 medium (fist-sized) potatoes, boiled and sliced
- 4 to 6 hardboiled eggs, cut in wedges
- 3 cakes tofu ~ plain or fried, diced
- a small handful each (if available):
   minced fresh cilantro, mint, and basil
- optional: a handful or two of mung bean sprouts
- FUN OPTION: potato chips instead of, or in addition to, the boiled potato slices
- squeezable wedges of lemon or lime, for garnish

Sri Wasano's Infamous Indonesian Rice Salad ☉

1) Place in a saucepan. Bring to a boil, lower heat, cover, and simmer until tender (35 to 45 minutes).

{ 2 cups brown rice
{ 3 cups water

2) While the rice cooks, combine in a large bowl:

⅓ cup peanut oil
3 Tbs. Chinese sesame oil
½ cup orange juice
1 to 2 medium cloves garlic, minced
1 tsp. salt
2 Tbs. soy sauce
½ tsp. crushed red pepper (to taste)
2 Tbs. rice or cider vinegar
1 cup chopped fresh pineapple (also ok
      to use canned-in-juice crushed pineapple)

3) Add the hot rice directly to the bowlful of dressing. Mix well. When it has cooled to room temperature, cover tightly and refrigerate until cold. Shortly before serving, stir in:

3 scallions, finely minced (whites and greens)
1 stalk celery, finely minced
1 medium-sized red or green bell pepper, thinly sliced
1 8-oz. can water chestnuts, drained & thinly sliced
½ lb. fresh mung bean sprouts
½ cup (packed) raisins or currants
1 cup coarsely chopped peanuts and/or cashews,
      lightly toasted
2 Tbs. sesame seeds
OPTIONAL: fresh snow peas, for garnish

Preparation time:
45 minutes to an hour
(depends on how
much stuff you
choose to put in)

Kristina's Potato Salad

Yield:
6 main dish portions
(more, if serving
with other things)

This is a kitchen-sink-type of potato salad, brimming with fresh vegetables, and texturally enhanced by the addition of toasted nuts and seeds. Make it as simple or as chock-full as you have time, ingredients, and desire for. Serve this salad as a main dish for a summer lunch, especially if paired with a chilled soup from the previous chapter.

Boil until tender; drain and cool.

{ 6 medium potatoes (about 3 lbs.), scrubbed, and chopped into 1½-inch pieces (that's approximate, of course)

2 hardboiled eggs, chopped

1 medium bell pepper (any color), diced

3 to 4 finely minced scallions (whites and greens)

1 small cucumber (peel if waxed), seeded and minced

1 cup (packed) finely minced parsley

¼ cup (packed) minced fresh dill (about 1 Tbs. dried)

1 to 2 tsp. salt (to taste)

fresh black pepper

¼ to ⅓ cup cider vinegar (possibly more, to taste)

1 to 2 tsp. dry mustard

1 to 2 tsp. tarragon

1 to 2 Tbs. prepared horseradish

½ to 1 cup mayonnaise (see recipe for homemade, including Tofu Mayo, p. 44 and Plain Fake Mayo, p. 91)

½ to 1 cup yogurt or sour cream

OPTIONAL ADDITIONS:

a handful of alfalfa sprouts

1 medium carrot, diced

1 stalk celery, minced

thinly sliced radishes

fresh peas, raw or steamed

1 cup lightly toasted cashews

½ cup toasted sunflower seeds

2 to 3 Tbs. sesame seeds

fresh spinach leaves ⎫
cherry tomatoes ⎬ for garnish
olives ⎭

Combine well, season to taste, cover, and chill.

Perfect Protein Salad

Crunchy cooked soybeans and chewy cooked wheat or rye berries are blended with minced fresh vegetables in a creamy lowfat dressing. A possibly interesting socio-historical note: I invented this recipe by default in 1973 while living in a house with about 10 other people. The ingredients of this salad— including a jar each of cooked soybeans and wheat berries—were the entire contents of our refrigerator. I just mixed them all together and behold, delicious!

The name was influenced by Frances Moore Lappé's first edition of <u>Diet for a Small Planet</u>, which I had just recently discovered at that time.

PRELIMINARILY: Soak the soybeans for at least 4 hours and the wheat or rye berries for at least 30 minutes. (Soaking them overnight is also fine.)

¾ cup dry soybeans, soaked
¾ cup dry wheat or rye berries, soaked
¼ to ⅓ cup cider vinegar (to taste)
1 tsp. salt
fresh black pepper, to taste
¼ cup minced fresh dill (or 2 tsp. dried)
¼ to ⅓ cup mayonnaise (see p. 44 and p. 91)

1 to 2 small cloves garlic, minced
½ cup finely minced parsley
1 cup cottage cheese or mashed tofu
3 scallions, finely minced
1 medium carrot, minced
1 small cucumber, peeled, seeded, and minced
a little bit of minced bell pepper

OPTIONAL: additional vegetables, such as minced red onion or celery, fresh alfalfa sprouts, sliced radish; fresh, ripe tomato slices, for garnish

1) Place the soaked soybeans in a medium-sized saucepan and cover with water. Place the soaked wheat or rye berries in another saucepan and add at least 2 cups of water. Bring each to a boil, partially cover, and simmer until tender. This will take between 1 and 1¼ hours. (You can also try just cooking them together in one large pot. Their cooking times are about the same.) When the soybeans are crunchy-but-tender, and the grains are chewy-but-tender, rinse them in a colander and drain well. Transfer to a medium-sized bowl.

2) Combine everything and mix well. Serve garnished with ripe tomato slices and behold, delicious!

How to Cut a Beautiful
FRUIT SALAD

If you just want to eat a piece of ripe, fresh fruit ~ or cut up a little assortment to serve to a few people ~ instructions are probably unnecessary. But the prospect of preparing a giant bowlful of freshly cut fruit (to serve to unpredictable numbers or just to have around for unlimited high-level snacking) can be daunting. Here, to undaunt you, are some tips which I hope will be encouraging and useful. Then you can regularly and confidently serve wonderful fruit medleys to volumes of appreciative friends, and everyone will want to come over to your house all the time.

ORANGES AND GRAPEFRUIT:

Use a sharp serrated knife. Cut the skin first from the polar ends, and then from the sides. (If you simply pull off the peel with your hands, citrus fruit will retain the inelegant white matter under the skin, which you probably don't want in your fruit salad.) Hold the peeled fruit over the bowl, and cut with a gentle sawing motion in and out along each membrane, releasing segments of fruit. You will end up holding a fanlike piece of juicy refuse. Squeeze all the juice from this unit into the bowl, and discard the remains. You will have before you a bowlful of captivating citrus sections.

PEACHES AND PLUMS; APPLES AND PEARS:

Make sure they are not over- or under-ripe. Cut in half first, take out the pit or seeds, and cut into slices or chunks just before serving. (If you want to cut them in advance, drizzle with lemon juice, and cover tightly.) Stir in gently as you serve.

PINEAPPLE:

You can tell if it's ripe by smelling it. Use a stainless steel knife to cut off the top and the bottom, then carve off the skin from the sides. Be sure to cut far enough into the pineapple to get off all the traces of prickly skin. It's preferable to lose a little of the goods than to accidentally get a thorn in the mouth. (People shouldn't have to examine each mouthful before eating it.) Cut the pineapple in half, then in quarters lengthwise. Cut the center core strip from each quarter, then chop the remaining fruit into 1-inch pieces.

WATERMELON:

The seeds of a watermelon grow in line patterns. Take your chunk of fruit salad-to-be and examine it to discover the pattern of seeds. Then take a teaspoon handle and pull it through the pattern to evict the seeds. When the seeds are mostly gone, chop the watermelon into 2- to 3-inch pieces. Don't make them too small, or they'll disintegrate.

MELONS OTHER THAN WATERMELON:

Use a stainless steel straight-bladed knife or a cleaver. Cut off the skin from each end, then stand the melon on one end, and carve off the skin from the sides. After the skin is off, cut in half and remove the seeds. Chop the remaining melon into 1-inch pieces.

CHERRIES AND BERRIES:

Halve and pit cherries, and mix them in, OR leave them whole and use to garnish the top. Cut larger berries in half; leave smaller ones whole. Mix in gently or lay decoratively on top.

BANANAS, PAPAYAS, MANGOS, KIWIS:

Make sure they are ripe, but not too, too soft. Peel, slice, and lay on top just before serving. (They will mush into oblivion if mixed in.) If you must cut these fruits ahead of time, sprinkle generously with lemon or lime juice.

DEAD-OF-WINTER FRUIT SALAD:

If you want to have a fruit salad in the off-season, and you'd like it to be more interesting than just apples and bananas, try using frozen unsweetened fruit. Plastic bags of various berries, pitted cherries, and sliced peaches can usually be found in the frozen foods section of larger supermarkets. Frozen berries give off delicious and deeply-hued juice as they defrost (empty the bag into a bowl while the fruit is still frozen), and the resulting fruit salad will be very juicy and a wonderful dark reddish-purple color.

In addition to defrosted frozen fruit, a winter fruit salad can also contain: citrus sections, pineapple (fresh or canned-in-juice), apples, pears, and bananas.

TOFU  SALAD

15 minutes to prepare
plus time to marinate

Yield: 6 servings

Unadulterated tofu is cloudlike and bland. Sometimes it's comforting, but sometimes it cries out for a little more action. This recipe calls for adulterating your tofu by marinating it in deep, strong flavors, which it readily absorbs. The crunchy vegetables provide a refreshing contrast.

This delicious salad gets more and more flavorful the longer it sits around, so go ahead and make it up to several days in advance.

The Marinade

4 Tbs. Chinese sesame oil
5 Tbs. rice or cider vinegar
1 Tbs. sugar
3 Tbs. soy sauce
optional: 1 to 2 Tbs. dry sherry or rice wine

2 to 3 medium cloves garlic, minced
½ tsp. salt (to taste)
crushed red pepper, to taste
optional: 1 tsp. minced fresh ginger

6 cakes (about 1 to 1½ lbs.) very firm tofu, well drained
8 to 10 medium-sized mushrooms
1 small carrot, shredded or cut into slender matchsticks
1 small bell pepper (preferably red), minced
optional: finely shredded cabbage
    1 to 2 minced scallions
    a handful or two of fresh mung bean sprouts
• optional toppings: • ½ cup coarsely chopped peanuts
    • minced fresh cilantro
    • diced fresh, ripe tomato
    • a sprinkling of sesame seeds

1) Combine marinade ingredients in a large, shallow bowl or pan.
2) Cut the tofu into ½-inch cubes and add to the marinade, along with the vegetables. Stir gently.
3) Cover and let marinate at room temperature for at least 2 hours. Serve cold or at room temperature, topped with all or some of the garnishes.

SERVING IDEAS: ☆ as a sandwich in Pita Bread (p. 113) with shredded cabbage and chopped tomatoes ☆ on hot rice, with Duck Sauce (p. 97) or Chinese Mustard (p. 120) ☆ in lettuce cups, with Chinese Green Onion Pancakes (p. 115) and either of the above-mentioned sauces.

Alsatian Salad

The original version of this dish was made with thinly cut cheese mixed with fresh vegetables in a creamy mustard dressing. Now that many people want to limit their cheese intake, I've added a Tofu Option, which is delicious! Use "savory baked" or "5-spice" tofu (a.k.a. "tofu kan"), both available in natural foods stores. Use either kind by itself, or in combination with very firm plain tofu.

Made with tofu or cheese, this is a wonderful lunch entrée.

1) Toss together very gently in a medium-sized bowl:

    3 cups cut cheese ~ in thin strips or in ½-inch cubes
      (Try a combination of cheddar and Swiss, or
      something smoked), OR:
    3 cups firm tofu strips
    1 small cucumber ~ peeled, seeded, and cut in thin strips
    1 bell pepper (any color), in small, thin strips
    1 minced scallion (include greens)
    OPTIONAL: ½ cup finely minced red onion

2) Combine well and add to cheese or tofu mixture:

½ cup yogurt	¼ to ½ tsp. each:
3 Tbs. mayonnaise (see recipes, p.44 + p.91)	paprika
1 small clove garlic, minced	basil
2 tsp. Dijon mustard	tarragon
½ tsp. prepared horseradish	dill
salt and pepper, to taste	a handful of minced parsley

GARNISHES:
fresh greens (small and leafy, like spinach or arugula)
cherry tomatoes (in the summer, look for yellow pear-shaped ones)
raw or steamed vegetables
pickles
olives
crusty bread

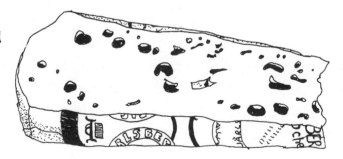

Four Waldorf Variations

A cross between a fruit and a vegetable salad, Waldorf Salad can be a first or second course for dinner. It also makes a good lunch entrée. Serve it on a bed of crispy lettuce, with thick slices of whole wheat toast.

♪♪ MAYONNAISE NOTES: Two of these variations have mayonnaise in the dressings. You can find recipes for homemade (regular or tofu-based) on p. 44 and p. 91.

I. BLUE MOON

2 medium-sized tart apples, in chunks
2 perfectly ripe pears (any kind), sliced
1 stalk celery, minced
¼ cup (packed) raisins
2 to 3 Tbs. lemon juice
¾ cup chopped toasted walnuts

Dressing:
1 cup yogurt
3 to 4 Tbs. mayonnaise
⅓ cup crumbled blue cheese
1 Tbs. honey (optional, to taste)

Combine all salad ingredients. Stir together dressing ingredients in a separate bowl, then pour over salad and gently mix.

II. CALIFORNIA

3 medium-sized tart and/or sweet apples
2 navel oranges, sectioned
1 stalk celery, minced
¼ cup (packed) raisins or currants
1 cup sliced ripe mango or papaya
   (optional, if available)
} for the top
1 cup toasted cashew pieces

Dressing:
1 cup yogurt
½ tsp. lemon rind
2 to 3 Tbs. lemon juice
1 ripe avocado, mashed
1 to 2 Tbs. honey (to taste)

Combine apples, oranges, celery, and raisins or currants. Purée together all dressing ingredients in a blender or food processor. Combine apple mixture with dressing and mix well. Serve topped with slices of ripe mango or papaya (if you're lucky enough to have some) and toasted cashews.

III. WALDORF DELUXE

3 medium-sized tart apples, in chunks
2 to 3 Tbs. lemon juice
1 stalk celery, minced
1 to 2 cups seedless grapes, whole or halved
     (optional)
1 cup diced cheddar
¼ cup (packed) minced dates
¾ cup chopped toasted pecans

Dressing:
1 cup yogurt
¼ cup mayonnaise
½ cup orange juice
½ tsp. grated orange rind

Combine salad ingredients. Whisk together dressing ingredients. Combine everything and mix well.

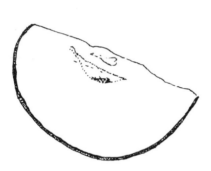

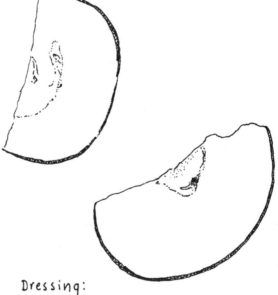

IV. FRUIT & VEGETABLE WALDORF

3 medium-sized tart apples, in chunks
1 cup freshly chopped pineapple
1 navel orange, sectioned
1 stalk celery, minced
1 small carrot, thinly sliced
1 red bell pepper, thinly sliced
¼ cup (packed) raisins or currants
½ to 1 cup chopped toasted almonds

Dressing:
1 cup yogurt
½ cup pineapple or orange juice
    (or a combination)
¼ tsp. cinnamon
a few dashes ground cardamom

Combine everything, and mix well.

Just White Beans

Preparation time:
1½ hours (mostly
bean-cooking time),
plus time to chill

Sometimes it's refreshing to have a bean salad that is a simple solo of lightly marinated beans, without a lot of little diced vegetables singing backup vocals. This is one such dish. It is delightful by itself, and down-right smashing when topped with a mound of Pickled Red Onions (see below).

This salad keeps well for days if tightly covered and refrigerated. The beans can be cooked without prior soaking.

1½ cups dry white pea beans
3 Tbs. olive oil
2 Tbs. red wine vinegar
¾ to 1 tsp. salt
1 to 2 medium cloves garlic, minced

freshly ground black pepper
½ tsp. basil
¼ cup finely minced parsley
2 Tbs. fresh (2 tsp. dried) dill
Pickled Red Onions (below)

1) Place the beans in a medium-sized saucepan and cover with water. Bring to a boil, reduce heat, and cook, partially covered until tender but not mushy (1 to 1¼ hours). Drain well, and transfer to a medium-sized bowl.
2) Add remaining ingredients, mix gently, and taste to correct seasonings. Cover tightly and chill until cold. Serve topped with Pickled Red Onions.

Pickled Red Onions

Try these with any bean salad, in or with sandwiches, in countless other salads, as an antipasto dish, or even on top of homemade pizza. Pickled Red Onions are ridiculously easy to make, and keep practically indefinitely.

1 cup cider vinegar
1 cup water
up to 3 Tbs. brown sugar

1 tsp. salt
1 tsp. whole peppercorns
4 medium red onions, very thinly sliced

PRELIMINARY: Fill a teakettle with water and put it up to boil.
1) Combine vinegar, 1 cup water, sugar, salt, and peppercorns in a medium-sized bowl and stir until the sugar is dissolved.
2) Place the onion slices in a colander in the sink, and slowly pour all the boiling water over them. They will wilt slightly. Drain well, and transfer to the bowlful of marinade.
3) Cover and allow to marinate, refrigerated or at room temperature, for at least several hours. Store in the refrigerator, and use as needed.

MULTI-BEAN SALAD

Presoaked beans need up to 1¼ hours to cook. (Get everything else ready during this time.) Allow at least a few hours to marinate.

Yield: 8 to 10 servings (possibly even more)

This festive and colorful salad is good with cornbread and any soup. Also, try serving it at room temperature over hot rice (you can melt some cheese into the rice) with steamed tortillas.

Try making this salad with a combination of 1 cup each: pinto, kidney, black, and garbanzo beans. Dry beans need to soak at least 4 hours – preferably overnight. Pinto, kidney, and black beans can be soaked, and then cooked, together. Garbanzos should be done separately.

4 cups dry beans, soaked
6 Tbs. olive oil
1 Tbs. minced garlic
3 to 4 Tbs. lemon juice
6 to 8 Tbs. red wine vinegar
1½ tsp. salt
lots of black pepper
¼ lb. fresh green beans

2 medium stalks celery, finely minced
⅓ cup very finely minced red onion
up to 1 cup (packed) finely minced parsley
1 small red or green bell pepper, minced
optional: a small amount of minced cucumber (peeled and seeded)
optional garnishes: cherry tomatoes
                    sieved hardboiled eggs

1) Cook presoaked beans in plenty of gently simmering water, partially covered, until just done. Keep the agitation to a minimum during the cooking, so the beans don't explode. Begin checking the beans for doneness at the 45-minute mark, just in case they are getting done early. The goal is: perfectly tender, distinct little morsels.
2) Combine oil, garlic, lemon juice, vinegar, salt, and pepper in a large bowl.
3) Trim the tips of the green beans, and steam until tender (5 to 8 minutes, or to your preference). Refresh under cold running water and drain well.
4) Drain the cooked beans and add them, still hot, to the bowlful of dressing. Add remaining ingredients and mix well. Let marinate for at least 2 or 3 hours (even longer is better).
5) Serve cold or at room temperature, garnished with cherry tomatoes, and, if desired, sieved hardboiled eggs.

Bermuda Salad

Yield: 4 to 6 servings,
depending on what goes
with it

~ marinated fresh whole green beans
and onion slices
with a touch of cheese ~

6 Tbs. olive oil
3 to 4 Tbs. red wine vinegar
1 ¼ tsp. salt
2 medium cloves garlic, minced
fresh black pepper, to taste
1 ½ cups thinly sliced red onion
3 cups boiling water
1 ½ lbs. fresh green beans, ends trimmed
1 to 2 cups (packed) mild or medium cheddar, grated
optional: about ½ cup finely minced parsley

1) Combine oil, vinegar, salt, garlic, and black pepper in a medium-sized bowl.

2) Place the sliced onion in a colander over the sink, and slowly douse it with 3 cups boiling water. Drain thoroughly, and transfer to the marinade, mixing well.

3) Steam the green beans until just tender, then immediately transfer to a colander and refresh them under cold running water. Drain well, and add to the marinade, along with the grated cheese (sprinkle it in as you mix gently). You can also throw in some finely minced parsley.

4) Marinate for at least several hours, either refrigerated or at room temperature, stirring occasionally. Serve cold or at room temperature.

About 45 minutes to prepare.
NOTE: You can do steps 1 + 2
a day or two in advance.

Yield:
approximately
6 to 8 servings

Marinated Vegetables

Delicately cooked vegetables, when marinated in a simple vinaigrette, make a festive and beautiful accompaniment to just about anything ~ or a light-but-filling main dish in their own right.

Steam the vegetables over water on the stove, or without water in the microwave. The following recipe is a sample method. Try substituting other vegetables ~ your favorites, or whatever is in season. Fresh or dry herbs can be used, depending on availability. Amounts are approximate and flexible.

1 medium cauliflower, in 1-inch pieces
1 medium bunch broccoli, cut in 2-inch stalks
2 medium carrots, sliced thin or in matchsticks
½ lb. mushrooms, sliced or quartered
1 small zucchini or yellow summer squash, in rounds
1 bell pepper (preferably red or yellow), thinly sliced
½ to ¾ cup olive oil
3 to 4 medium cloves garlic, minced
1 tsp. salt (maybe more later, to taste)
freshly ground black pepper
HERBS: (up to 1 tsp. if using dried; up to several Tbs. if using fresh):
   oregano or marjoram
   dill
   basil   optional and flexible
   chives   ~in other words, to taste
   thyme
OPTIONAL ADDITIONS: red onion slices (very thin), cooked beans, marinated artichoke hearts, minced scallions, raw sugar snap or snow peas, small cubes of mild white cheese or firm tofu
⅓ cup balsamic and/or red wine vinegar
GARNISHES: olives, hardboiled egg slices, cherry tomatoes, feta cheese

1) Steam the vegetables until just tender in the following groupings: cauliflower + broccoli + carrots; mushrooms + zucchini; bell pepper.
2) Meanwhile, combine oil, garlic, salt, pepper, and herbs in a large bowl. Add the steamed vegetables (ok if still hot) and whatever optional additions you may opt to add. Mix well.
3) Stir in vinegar within 30 minutes of serving. (Minimizing exposure to vinegar helps the vegetables retain their bright colors.)

ANTIPASTO

"Antipasto" is a broad term referring to the first of several courses served in a traditional Italian meal. This can mean a simple dish or two of sliced tomatoes or marinated beans or vegetables, or an elaborate platter of cold sliced meats and cheeses.

In this section, I've put together a variety of vegetable preparations, all of which are very simple, and when served all (or partially) together with fresh bread or breadsticks, olives, a small platter of fruit and cheese, and a bottle of red wine can make a complete and elegant light meal.

All of the following can be made up to several days in advance, and are good served either cold or at room temperature. Leftovers go beautifully as toppings or garnishes for green salads, or as accompaniments to simple pasta dinners. "Antipasto servings" translates to "modest-sized, side-dish-type servings."

Gingery Marinated Chick Peas

Preparation time: Presoaked chick peas need about 1½ hrs. to cook; everything else takes only about 10 minutes.

Yield: about 5 cups

This tastes best when made several days ahead (it gets better and better). Keep a batch around to put on top of green salads, or to serve mixed with hot rice, or by itself as an antipasto.

NOTE: You can use canned chick peas if you're in a pinch (rinse and drain them very well). Use 5 cups.

3 cups dry chick peas (soaked at least
4 hours) cooked until tender (1¼ to 1½ hours)

5 to 6 Tbs. olive oil
3 to 4 Tbs. lemon juice
1 to 2 large cloves garlic, minced
1 to 2 Tbs. finely minced ginger

2 to 3 Tbs. red wine vinegar
1 tsp. salt
½ cup finely minced red onion
freshly ground black pepper

1) Rinse and thoroughly drain the cooked chick peas.

2) Combine everything, mix well, cover tightly, and let marinate practically indefinitely. Stir from the bottom periodically during marination.

15 minutes to prepare; 40 minutes to cook.

marinated small Artichokes

6 antipasto servings

Sure, you could just open a jar, but these are a whole different animal, if you'll pardon the expression, and almost as easy. Really!

Use small artichokes (2-inch diameter or less). Unlike larger artichokes, in which the rough parts and the choke have had a chance to develop, little ones require only minimal trimming, and are otherwise completely edible.

1½ lbs. small artichokes	⅓ cup olive oil
3 cups water	1½ tsp. salt
juice from 1 medium-sized lemon	1 tsp. whole peppercorns
⅓ cup red wine vinegar	4 medium cloves garlic, peeled

1) Cut off the tips and stems of the artichokes. Shave off any extraneous outer leaves with scissors or a paring knife. You can leave the artichokes whole or cut them lengthwise into smaller chunks ~ whatever seems more appealing.

2) Combine everything in a saucepan. Bring to a boil, lower heat to medium, and gently boil, uncovered, until the liquid reduces to approximately 1 cup. This will take 30 to 40 minutes.

3) Remove from heat and cool to room temperature. This will keep for several weeks if stored in a tightly covered container in the refrigerator. Serve cold or at room temperature.

Preparation time: 15 minutes

Bell Peppers

Yield: about 6 antipasto servings

6 medium-sized bell peppers (try to get a mix of colors)	½ tsp. marjoram or oregano
	fresh black pepper, to taste
2 Tbs. olive oil	2 medium cloves garlic, minced
½ tsp. salt	
½ to 1 tsp. basil	1 to 2 Tbs. red wine vinegar

1) Stem and seed the peppers, then cut them into thin strips.

2) Heat olive oil in a heavy skillet. Add peppers, salt, herbs, and black pepper. Cook, stirring over medium heat for about 5 minutes. Then add garlic. Sauté another few minutes, or until the peppers are just tender.

3) Remove from heat, and immediately stir in the vinegar. Let marinate at room temperature for at least an hour. Store in the refrigerator, tightly covered. Serve at any temperature.

Cauliflower & Carrots

15 minutes to prepare

Yield: 6
antipasto servings

1 to 2 Tbs. olive oil
4 cups small (1-inch) cauliflowerets
3 medium carrots, in thin 1½-inch strips
½ tsp. salt (more, to taste)
2 large cloves garlic, minced

1 to 3 Tbs. balsamic vinegar
  (to taste)
fresh black pepper
OPTIONAL: a few leaves of
  fresh basil, cut in strips

1) Heat olive oil in a medium-sized skillet. Add cauliflower, carrots, and salt, and sauté over medium heat until tender (8 to 10 minutes). Stir in garlic during the last few minutes of cooking.

2) Transfer to a bowl; add vinegar, black pepper, and optional basil. Serve warm, cold, or at room temperature.

Preparation time:
  20 minutes

Swiss Chard

Yield: 4 to 6
antipasto servings

The following instructions are for preparing the chard in two batches, as it is quite bulky until it cooks down. If you have a very large wok or skillet, you might be able to fit it all into one effort.

1½ lbs. Swiss chard (ruby and/or green)
2 to 3 Tbs. olive oil
6 medium cloves garlic, minced
salt and pepper, to taste
2 Tbs. balsamic or red wine vinegar

1) Coarsely chop the chard (include as much of the stems as feasible.)

2) Heat a wok or a large heavy skillet. Add 1 Tbs. olive oil and half the chard. Turn up the heat, and stir-fry for several minutes. When the chard begins to be limp, add half the garlic, and stir-fry for just a few minutes more.

3) Transfer to a platter or bowl. Sprinkle lightly with salt, heavily with pepper, and toss with 1 Tbs. vinegar.

4) Repeat with the remaining half of the ingredients. Taste to adjust seasonings. (You may wish to add a little more olive oil.) Serve hot, cold, or at room temperature.

Marinated Mushrooms

Preparation time:
25 minutes

Yield: 4 to 6
antipasto servings

1 lb. small mushrooms (1-inch diameter)
3 Tbs. olive oil
1 to 2 Tbs. lemon juice
½ tsp. salt
¼ to ½ tsp. thyme
1 medium clove garlic, minced
fresh black pepper
a handful of finely minced parsley

1) Clean the mushrooms thoroughly, slicing off and discarding the stems. Place the mushroom caps in a saucepan with no added water, cover, and cook them over medium heat 10 to 15 minutes.

2) Meanwhile, prepare the marinade by combining all the remaining ingredients in a medium-small bowl.

3) Drain the mushrooms. (For a great soup stock, reserve the liquid.) Place the mushrooms in the marinade, stir gently, and let marinate, either refrigerated or at room temperature, for at least several hours. Stir occasionally during marination. Serve cold or at room temperature.

Roasted Green Beans
with garlic & pine nuts

Preparation time:
30 to 40 minutes,
including roasting

Yield: 6
antipasto servings

2 Tbs. olive oil
1 lb. fresh whole green beans, trimmed
1 cup thinly sliced onion
10 to 12 medium cloves garlic, peeled
salt and pepper
1 to 2 Tbs. balsamic or red wine vinegar
1 cup lightly toasted pine nuts

1) Preheat oven to 400°F. Brush a large baking tray with 2 Tbs. olive oil.

2) Spread the green beans, onions, and garlic cloves on the tray and sprinkle lightly with salt and pepper.

3) Bake for 20 minutes, intermittently stirring or shaking the tray. Taste a green bean to see if it's as tender as you like it. If not, put it back in for another 5 or 10 minutes.

4) Remove from oven; transfer to a bowl. Drizzle with vinegar, and possibly grind in some additional black pepper. Serve at any temperature, topped with lightly toasted pine nuts.

Odessa Beets

Preparation time: The beets
need 45 minutes to bake;
after that, about 10 minutes

Yield: 6 or more
servings

Except for its special guest ingredient, pineapple, this recipe is authentically Ukrainian. Traditional versions might have even more garlic and a little mayonnaise. You can try it that way if it sounds good to you.

Odessa Beets keep beautifully for at least a week. Serve them alongside just about anything, even as an accompaniment to other salads. Try using this recipe as a stuffing in baked acorn squash, or as a side dish with Solyanka (p.136). You can put it in a salad sandwich (p.119) or just eat it straight. Even if you think you hate beets, there's a good chance you will love this salad.

5 to 6 medium beets (2- to 2½-inch diameter)
2 to 3 Tbs. lemon juice
8 to 10 prunes, pitted and thinly sliced
2 to 3 medium cloves garlic, minced
½ tsp. salt
black pepper, to taste
½ cup finely chopped walnuts
1 cup finely chopped pineapple (fresh or
        canned-in-juice)

1) Preheat oven to 400°F. Wrap the beets in foil and bake until very tender (40 to 45 minutes). Rinse under cold running water as you rub off the skins. Trim the ends and coarsely grate. (A food processor fitted with the grating attachment does this in seconds.) Transfer to a medium-sized bowl.

2) Add all remaining ingredients and mix well. Chill until serving time.

Balkan Cucumber Salad

Preparation time:　　　a delicious, refreshing, very easy salad　　　Yield:
10 to 15 minutes　　　　　　　　　　　　　　　　　　　　　　6 servings

½ cup very thinly sliced red onion
4 medium cucumbers (6 to 7 inches long)
1 tsp. salt
freshly ground black pepper
1½ cups yogurt
1 or 2 small cloves garlic, minced
1 to 2 tsp. honey (optional)
2 Tbs. freshly minced mint leaves (or 2 tsp. dried)
¼ cup (packed) finely minced parsley
2 scallions, finely minced (greens included)
1 to 2 Tbs. freshly minced dill (or 1 to 2 tsp. dried)
1 cup chopped walnuts, lightly toasted

1) Soak the onion in cold water for about 30 minutes while you get everything else ready. Drain thoroughly and pat dry before adding to the salad.

2) Peel (unless they're homegrown or unwaxed, in which case, don't) the cucumbers, seed them, and cut them into thin rounds. Place them in a medium-sized bowl.

3) Add remaining ingredients except walnuts, and mix well. Cover and refrigerate until serving time.

4) Sprinkle the walnuts on top just before serving.

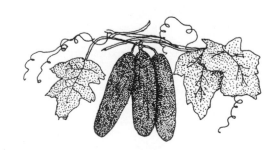

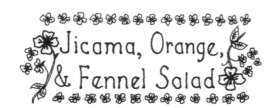

Jicama, Orange, & Fennel Salad

20 to 30 minutes to prepare

Yield: 4 to 6 servings

❀ Jicama ("hee-ca-ma") is a Mexican tuber that looks like a light brown turnip. It is incomparably crisp and fresh-tasting as a snack, and goes beautifully with dips. If you can't find it, substitute sunchoke or radish.

❀ Serve this salad as a second course, in place of dessert. It is so satisfying and refreshing, all yearnings for a sugary follow-up will instantly fade.

4 navel oranges
1 jicama (or a piece of one), about
   the size of a medium apple
1 small fennel bulb (2- to 3-inch diameter)
a few sprigs of arugula, if available
about 10 leaves of Belgian endive – OR–
   a handful of fresh spinach

DRESSING:
4 Tbs. olive oil
2 Tbs. orange juice
2 Tbs. balsamic or wine vinegar
2 tsp. raspberry vinegar (optional)
1 medium clove garlic, minced
½ tsp. salt
2 tsp. honey

optional garnish: Pickled Red Onions (p. 60)

1) Cut off the ends of the oranges with a sharp serrated knife, then slice the peel from the sides. With a gentle sawing motion, cut along each membrane to release the orange sections into a small bowl. Set aside.

2) Peel the jicama, and cut into very thin slices about 1½ inches long. Slice the fennel into very thin strips; include the feathery tops. Chop the arugula.

3) In a small bowl, whisk together the dressing ingredients until the honey is dissolved. Refrigerate everything until serving time.

4) Assemble the salad on a small platter shortly before serving. First, put down a layer of endive or spinach (a starburst pattern looks real nice), then a layer of jicama slices. Drizzle on some of the dressing, then sprinkle on fennel and arugula. Arrange orange sections on top, and spoon on a little more dressing. Garnish, if you are so inclined, with a few slices of Pickled Red Onion.

Marinated Sweet Potatoes & Broccoli

15 to 20 minutes to prepare;
at least 2 hours to marinate

Yield: about 6 servings

3 medium-sized sweet potatoes (1½ to 2 lbs.)

MARINADE:
½ cup walnut oil (if unavailable, use olive oil)
1 large clove garlic, minced
3 Tbs. lemon juice
2 Tbs. raspberry vinegar (if unavailable, use red wine vinegar)
1 to 1½ tsp. salt
1 Tbs. dry mustard
1 Tbs. honey
freshly ground black pepper

1 large bunch broccoli (1 to 1½ lbs.), cut into small spears

OPTIONAL GARNISHES: thin slices of green apple
                     chopped, toasted pecans

1) Peel the sweet potatoes, cut them in halves or quarters, then into thin slices. Put them up to cook, either in or over boiling water (in a steamer). Meanwhile, prepare the marinade.

2) Combine the marinade ingredients in a medium-large bowl. As soon as the sweet potato slices are tender, add them, still hot, to the marinade. Mix gently.

3) Steam the broccoli until bright green and just tender. Rinse under cold running water and drain completely. Lay the broccoli spears carefully on top of the salad. Cover tightly and marinate for several hours.

4) Within 15 minutes of serving, mix in the broccoli from on top. Serve garnished with thin slices of green apple and chopped, toasted pecans.

Carrot-Yogurt Salad

Preparation Time:
10 minutes (w/ food processor); 20 minutes (by hand)

Yield: 4 to 5 main-dish servings for lunch. More, if serving as a side dish.

1 lb. carrots, peeled and coarsely grated
2 medium-sized tart apples, grated
1 to 2 Tbs. lemon juice
1 to 2 Tbs. honey (optional)
pinch of celery seed
salt and pepper to taste
1 cup firm yogurt
OPTIONAL ADDITIONS:
1 Tbs. poppy seeds or toasted sesame seeds
¼ cup minced almonds or cashews, lightly toasted
½ cup very finely minced celery
a handful of raisins or currants
¼ cup shredded unsweetened coconut, lightly toasted
½ to 1 cup finely chopped pineapple (or crushed canned-in-juice)

Combine all ingredients and mix well. Chill. (This preparation goes fast if you use a food processor with the grating attachment.)

COLESLAW VARIATION

Same as above, but with the following alterations:
1) Substitute 4 cups shredded cabbage plus 2 large carrots for the 1 lb. carrots.
2) Apples = optional.
3) Substitute cider vinegar for the lemon juice.
4) You can use half yogurt and half mayonnaise. (Recipes for homemade mayo are on p. 44 and p. 91)
5) Add ½ cup each: minced green pepper and red onion.
6) Same Optional Additions.

SAUCES
AND
DIPS

CONTENTS: SAUCES AND DIPS

Pasta Sauces

This, plus the next 10 pages, contain ideas for pasta sauces, some traditional (Italian Tomato Sauce plus variations, Pesto, etc.), and some more unusual (Caramelized Onions, Stellar Mushroom Sauce, and more). I've tried to include some very easy and quick ideas, as well as a few more complex ones, so you can have a choice (and have lots of pasta in your life! There's nothing like a good plateful on a regular basis.)

These recipes assume you are using dried pasta. If you are using fresh, increase the amount of uncooked pasta by 50%. (So if the recipe calls for 1 lb. pasta, use 1½ lbs. fresh.) For a delicious and nutritious departure, try using cooked spaghetti squash sometimes, instead of pasta. Substitute 1 large (9- to 10-inch-long) squash, baked or boiled, for 1 lb. pasta.

TWO ULTRA-QUICK & EASY PASTA IDEAS

-For when you have no time to cook, and you need dinner Right Now.

1) <u>with Olive Oil, Garlic, Crushed Red Pepper, and Parmesan:</u>
 - Cook pasta.
 - Mince or crush some fresh garlic in the meantime.
 - Drain the pasta, drizzle it with olive oil, stir in the garlic and some crushed red pepper, to taste.
 - Sprinkle in some parmesan, and if you are slightly ambitious, top with a little minced parsley.

2) <u>with Marinated Artichoke Hearts from a Jar:</u>
 For every 2 people:
   ½ lb. pasta (smallish shells, ziti, fusilli, or penne = best)
   1 6-oz. jar marinated artichoke crowns or hearts
   parmesan
   black pepper
 - While the pasta cooks, drain the artichoke marinade into a serving bowl.
 - Cut the hearts or crowns into bite-sized pieces, and add to the bowl.
 - Add the drained pasta to the bowl, and toss. Serve immediately, passing the parmesan and a pepper mill.

Simplest Primavera

Pasta Primavera is a pasta-and-vegetable dish named in honor of the spring season. Ideally, it is full of the vegetable garden's earliest offerings. In keeping with that spirit, this simple version is made from the season's first greens: peas, scallions, herbs, and leafy greens.

....

1 lb. sugar snap or snow peas
5 or 6 scallions
4 Tbs. olive oil
OPTIONAL: 1 lb. leafy greens (kale, collard, or mustard),
       stemmed and coarsely chopped
½ tsp. salt
4 to 5 large cloves garlic, minced
a handful of fresh basil leaves, coarsely chopped (if
       unavailable, use parsley)
black pepper, to taste
½ lb. penne or fusilli (tube- or corkscrew-shaped pasta)
extra olive oil for the pasta
parmesan for the top   ....

1) Trim the peas at both ends, remove the strings, and cut the pods in half across the middle (unless they're very small, in which case, leave them whole).
2) Cut the scallions in half lengthwise, then into 1½-inch pieces.
3) Put up the pasta water to boil. Cook the pasta while you sauté the vegetables.
4) Heat the olive oil in a large wok or skillet. If you are using the greens, add these first, along with the salt. Sauté for about 5 minutes over high heat, then turn heat down, and add peas, scallions, and garlic. Sauté for 5 minutes more. Stir in the basil (or parsley) and black pepper during the last minute or so. (If you are not using the greens, just begin the sauté with the peas, scallions, and garlic.)
5) When the pasta is done, drain it (or scoop it out of the hot water with a strainer or a slotted pasta scooper), and add it directly to the vegetables in the wok or skillet. Sauté the pasta with the vegetables for 2 or 3 minutes — until everything is fully mingled — and serve immediately. Pass a cruet of olive oil and some parmesan.

asparagus~mushroom sauce

Although designed for pasta, this sauce is also good in Crêpes (p. 142) or on rice or baked fish. If you have some left over, try filling an omelette with it.

1½ lbs. fresh asparagus — slender as possible, trimmed
     at the bottom and cut into 2-inch spears
2 Tbs. butter
1½ cups minced onion
1 tsp. salt
1 lb. mushrooms, sliced
½ tsp. tarragon
black pepper, to taste
1½ cups dry white wine
1 cup water
1 to 2 Tbs. flour (depending on how thick you like it)
6 to 8 cloves garlic, minced
½ to ¾ lb. pasta (any shape)
olive oil or extra butter for the pasta
parmesan for the top
minced fresh dill (optional)

1) Steam the asparagus until just tender. Transfer to a colander over a sink and refresh under cold running water. Drain well and set aside.

2) Melt the butter in a large skillet. Add onion and salt, and sauté for about 5 minutes. Add mushrooms, tarragon, and pepper.
Cover and cook over medium heat for 15 minutes, stirring occasionally.

3) Add wine and water. Turn up heat until the liquid boils. Sprinkle in the flour, whisking constantly until it completely dissolves. Lower heat, cover, and simmer about 10 minutes, stirring frequently. Add garlic, and cook about 5 minutes more. Set aside until serving time.

4) Gently reheat the sauce while you cook the pasta. Stir the steamed asparagus into the sauce at the last minute. Toss the drained pasta with a little olive oil or butter, and serve topped with sauce, parmesan, and possibly a little freshly minced dill.

PASTA WITH
Caramelized Onion Sauce

The proportions of ingredients in this delicious recipe are somewhat flexible. You can play with the amounts of onions and greens, and you can substitute other leafy greens (collard, escarole, mustard, etc.) for the arugula or spinach. Other soft pungent cheeses can be substituted for the feta or blue cheese.

NOTE: The alcoholic content of the wine will dissipate with cooking.

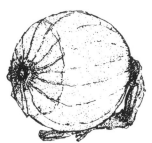

½ cup olive oil
4 to 6 large onions (however many you have the patience to slice), thinly sliced (about 6 to 8 cups)
½ tsp. salt
½ to 1 cup dry white wine
1 medium bunch arugula or spinach, stemmed and minced

1 cup crumbled feta or blue cheese
¾ lb. pasta (a short, shapely variety, like penne or fusilli)

1 cup chopped, toasted walnuts
parmesan

1) Heat olive oil in a large skillet or sauté pan. Add onions, and sauté over medium heat for about 15 minutes. Add salt, lower heat, and continue to cook for at least another 10 minutes (and up to an hour for really deliciously well-done onions).

2) Add white wine, turn heat back up to medium, and simmer uncovered for about 15 minutes. At this point the sauce can be set aside until you are ready to cook the pasta.

3) Turn the heat back on under the sauce when you are ready to cook the pasta. When the onions are hot, add the chopped greens, stir, and cook for about 5 minutes. Stir in the crumbled cheese, and turn heat to low while cooking the pasta.

4) After the cooked pasta is drained, add it to the sauce, and stir briefly in the pan before serving. Sprinkle with walnuts and parmesan, and serve.

PASTA WITH

Stellar Mushroom Sauce

2 oz. dried Chinese black mushrooms

2 Tbs. butter
1 lb. domestic mushrooms, chopped
3/4 lb. fresh shiitake, oyster, and/or
   chanterelle mushrooms, chopped
1 cup minced onion
1 tsp. salt

6 Tbs. dry sherry
3 Tbs. flour
1/2 to 3/4 lb. pasta (any shape)
1 large clove garlic, minced
black pepper, to taste
1/2 cup sour cream, at
   room temperature
parmesan for the top

1) PRELIMINARY: Place the dried mushrooms in a bowl. Add 2 cups boiling water, cover with a plate, and let stand 30 minutes. Drain the mushrooms in a cheesecloth-lined strainer over a bowl, squeezing out and saving all the liquid. Remove and discard the stems; coarsely chop the mushrooms. Measure out 2/3 cup of the liquid to use in this recipe. (Save any remaining liquid to use as a delicious soup stock.)

2) Put up some pasta water to boil. Melt butter in a deep skillet or Dutch oven. Add all mushrooms, the onions, and the salt. Cook uncovered over medium heat for 10 minutes. Stir in the sherry.

3) Turn heat to low, and have a whisk ready. Slowly sprinkle in the flour, whisking steadily. Keep whisking for a minute or two after all the flour is in. Meanwhile, begin cooking the pasta.

4) Add garlic and black pepper; continue cooking/stirring for 10 minutes.

5) Stir in the sour cream and the 2/3 cup reserved mushroom-soaking liquid from Step 1, mixing well until incorporated.

6) Drain the pasta, transfer to serving plates, and spoon a generous amount of sauce on top. Sprinkle with parmesan, and serve.

ITALIAN TOMATO SAUCE

The classic red sauce, without meat, and with 2 variations. Use any version of this in Lasagne (p. 132) or Eggplant Parmesan (p. 133), or on pasta of any size or shape.

Make a full batch even if you won't use it all in one meal. All of these variations keep well up to a week in the refrigerator, and much longer in the freezer.

2 to 3 Tbs. olive oil	1 1-lb., 13-oz. can tomatoes
2 cups chopped onion	1 6-oz. can tomato paste
1 medium-sized bell pepper, diced	1 Tbs. honey
2 tsp. basil	lots of black pepper
1 tsp. oregano	4 to 6 large cloves garlic, minced
1 tsp. thyme	
1½ tsp. salt	½ cup freshly minced parsley

1) Heat the olive oil in a Dutch oven or kettle. Add onion, bell pepper, herbs, and salt, and sauté over medium heat until the onion is very soft (8 to 10 minutes).

2) Add tomatoes, tomato paste, honey, and black pepper. Use a spoon to break up the tomatoes into bite-sized pieces. Bring to a boil, then lower heat and simmer, partially covered, for 20 to 30 minutes.

3) Add garlic, and cook about 10 minutes more. At this point, the sauce can sit for up to several hours, or be refrigerated for up to a week. Heat gently before serving, and add parsley at the last minute.

MARINARA VARIATION:

2 medium stalks celery, minced
1 lb. mushrooms, chopped
1 to 2 medium (6-inch) zucchini, diced
2 to 3 medium-sized ripe tomatoes, chopped
a handful of fresh basil leaves, chopped

} Add with step 1. Sauté until all vegetables are very tender.

CAVOLFIORE VARIATION:

1 large cauliflower, in 1-inch florets

} Steam until tender. Add to Step 2.

🍅 Sauce Puttanesca 🍅

🍅 🍅 🍅 🍅 🍅 🍅 🍅 🍅 🍅 🍅 🍅 🍅 🍅 🍅

... intensely seasoned tomato sauce with a special guest star: the much-maligned but ever spunky anchovy. Of course, if you are a strict, not-even-fish vegetarian, this addition will be out of the question, and the sauce will still taste fine without it. But if you are a fish-eater, try the anchovies, even if you must overcome a degree of prejudice to do so. You will find that their flavor blends in surprisingly well.

This sauce is quick and easy — it doesn't require prolonged simmering—so you can whip it up after a busy day of work. Serve over any shape of pasta, accompanied by a green salad and some fresh crusty bread.

1 1-lb., 13-oz. can whole or crushed tomatoes
1 6-oz. can tomato paste
10 to 12 medium cloves garlic, thinly sliced
15 to 20 Kalamata (Greek) olives, carved off the pit and sliced
OPTIONAL: 3 to 4 anchovies, minced — OR— 1 to 2 Tbs.
          anchovy paste (can be increased, to taste)
black pepper   } to taste
crushed red pepper }
¾ to 1 lb. pasta (any shape)
olive oil for the pasta
parmesan
freshly minced parsley
for PASTA MEDITERRANÉE: 1 cup crumbled feta cheese

PRELIMINARY: Put up pasta water to boil.
1) For a smoother sauce, purée the tomatoes in their liquid in a blender or food processor. For a chunkier sauce, cut the tomatoes into chunks with a knife, saving the liquid. (Skip this step if using crushed tomatoes.)
2) Combine tomatoes, their liquid, tomato paste, garlic, olives, and anchovies in a medium-sized saucepan, and gradually heat to a boil. Reduce heat, season to taste with black and crushed red pepper, and simmer about 10 minutes. (You can cook the pasta during this time.)
3) Drain the pasta, and toss with a little olive oil. Add the sauce, and serve immediately, topped with parmesan and parsley (and feta cheese, if desired).

Broccoli Sauce
for Pasta

During the height of the produce season, you can make this lovely dish particularly colorful by pairing a yellow bell pepper with red cherry tomatoes — or a red bell pepper with yellow cherry tomatoes.

If you can't find Niçoise olives, use Kalamata (Greek) olives, carved off the pit and sliced. If using Niçoise olives, remind your guests to watch out for the pits.

3 Tbs. olive oil
2 cups chopped onion
1 1½-lb. bunch broccoli, in 1½-inch pieces
1 tsp. salt
1 red or yellow bell pepper, cut into 1½-inch strips
2 cups water or vegetable broth
2 Tbs. flour
2 cups cherry tomatoes, halved
½ cup Niçoise olives
6 large cloves garlic, minced

½ to ¾ lb. pasta (any shape)
Extra olive oil for the pasta
Parmesan } for the top
Black pepper }

OPTIONAL ADDITIONS:
○ Sun-dried tomatoes, softened in hot water and chopped
○ A few dried mushrooms, softened in hot water and sliced
○ A handful of lightly toasted pine nuts

PRELIMINARY: Put up some pasta water to boil.

1) Heat the olive oil in a large, deep skillet or Dutch oven. Add the onion, and sauté over medium heat until very soft (10 to 15 minutes).
2) Add broccoli and salt, and sauté another 10 minutes or so — until the broccoli is just tender.
3) Add the bell pepper, stir, and sauté about 5 minutes longer.
4) Add water or broth, and turn up the heat until it boils. Lower heat to medium, and sprinkle in the flour, whisking until dissolved.
5) Stir in the tomatoes, olives, garlic, and optional sun-dried tomatoes and/or mushrooms. Keep the sauce warm while you cook the pasta.
6) Drain the pasta, toss it with a little extra olive oil, and transfer to a serving dish. Pour/spoon in the sauce, and sprinkle with parmesan, black pepper, and optional pine nuts. Serve hot.

Eggplant Scallopini Marsala } For Pasta

Preparation time: 45 minutes

Yield: about 4 to 5 servings

OPTIONAL PRELIMINARY: To peel and seed the tomatoes, heat a medium-sized potful of water, then lower heat to a simmer. Core the tomatoes, then drop them into the water for about 10 seconds. Retrieve them, pull off and discard the skins, then cut the tomatoes in half. Squeeze out the seeds, and chop the remaining pulp.

- 2 to 3 Tbs. olive oil
- 2 cups chopped onion
- 2 bay leaves
- 6 cups diced eggplant (about 1 large eggplant) (peeling optional)
- 2 medium-sized bell peppers, any color, diced
- 1 lb. mushrooms, chopped
- 2 tsp. salt
- 2 tsp. dried basil (or 2 Tbs. minced fresh)
- 1 cup marsala or dry sherry
- 3 to 4 medium-sized ripe tomatoes, chopped (Peeling and seeding = optional. See "optional preliminary" above.)
- Black pepper, to taste
- 10 medium cloves garlic, minced
- ½ to ¾ lb. pasta (any shape)
- Additional olive oil for the pasta
- Parmesan } for the top
- Minced parsley }

1) Put up some water to boil for the pasta. Meanwhile, heat the olive oil in a deep skillet or Dutch oven. Add onion and bay leaves, and sauté over medium heat until the onions soften (5 to 8 minutes).
2) Add eggplant, peppers, mushrooms, salt, and basil. Cover and cook until the eggplant is tender (10 to 15 minutes), stirring occasionally.
3) Add marsala or sherry, tomatoes, and black pepper. Simmer uncovered for 10 to 15 minutes. (The liquid will reduce.) Stir in the garlic during the last 5 minutes. Meanwhile, cook the pasta.
4) Drain the pasta and transfer to a serving dish. Drizzle and toss with a little extra olive oil, and spoon the eggplant mixture on top. Sprinkle with parmesan and parsley, and serve hot.

Pesto

This most-famous potent, green version of pesto features basil, garlic, and olive oil. When tossed with hot pasta (especially long, thin varieties, like spaghetti or linguine), it adheres to each available surface, coating the pasta with intense flavor. This pesto keeps for weeks, or even months, if stored in a tightly lidded sterile jar in the refrigerator.

3 cups (packed) fresh basil leaves
3 to 4 large cloves garlic
optional: ⅓ cup pine nuts or chopped walnuts, lightly toasted

⅓ cup olive oil
⅓ cup parmesan
optional: salt and pepper, to taste

1) Place the basil leaves and garlic in a blender or food processor and mince.
2) Add the nuts, if desired, and continue to blend until the nuts are ground.
3) Drizzle in the olive oil, as you keep the machine running. When you have a smooth paste, transfer to a bowl, and stir in the parmesan. Season to taste with salt and pepper. To serve, place room-temperature Pesto in a warmed serving bowl. Add hot pasta and toss thoroughly. Allow 2 to 3 Tbs. Pesto per serving.

MONDO BIZARRO SAUCE

Tomato-spinach pesto for pasta

This sauce is especially good on pasta with Ricotta Gnocchi (next recipe).
To peel and seed tomatoes: Drop them into simmering water for 10 seconds. Then retrieve them, and pull off the skins. Cut them open; squeeze out and discard the seeds.

4 or 5 large cloves garlic
⅓ cup fresh basil leaves
⅓ cup minced parsley
1 1-lb. bunch spinach, stemmed
2 to 3 medium-sized ripe tomatoes, peeled and seeded (see above)

½ cup parmesan, plus extra, for the top
½ tsp. salt
optional: ½ cup pine nuts or finely minced walnuts, lightly toasted
freshly ground black pepper
optional: olive oil for the pasta

Continued →

1) Place the garlic, basil, parsley, and spinach in a food processor or blender, and work into a uniform paste.

2) Add the tomatoes, and process just a few seconds more. Transfer to a bowl, and stir in parmesan, salt, and optional nuts (or save these for sprinkling on top).

3) Serve the room-temperature sauce with hot pasta (and possibly Ricotta Gnocchi) in a warmed serving bowl. Pass some extra parmesan, the pepper grinder, and if desired, a cruet of olive oil.

Ricotta Gnocchi

Preparation time:
30 minutes

Yield: about 2
dozen dumplings

Serve these savory cheese dumplings as an appetizer or with pasta. You can make and poach them ahead of time. Broil just before serving.

½ lb. mozzarella cheese	2 eggs	Black pepper, to taste
1 large handful parsley	½ tsp. salt	A little butter or olive
2 large cloves garlic	¼ cup parmesan	oil for the pan
1 lb. ricotta cheese	1¼ cups flour	Extra parmesan for the top

1) Fill a large kettle with water and put it up to boil.

2) Meanwhile, grate the mozzarella (the grating attachment of a food processor does this fast) and transfer to a medium-sized bowl.

3) Mince the parsley and garlic — either by hand or in the food processor — and stir this into the grated cheese.

4) Beat together the ricotta and eggs. (You can use the food processor.) Add this to the first mixture, with salt, parmesan, flour, and black pepper. Mix well.

5) When the water boils, reduce heat to a simmer, and drop in small blobs of batter (1 Tbs. each). Simmer for 15 minutes, then remove with a slotted spoon. The gnocchi will be soft. Refrigerate until 15 minutes before serving.

6) Shortly before serving, heat the broiler. Brush a baking dish with soft butter or olive oil, and arrange the gnocchi in the dish. Sprinkle with parmesan, and broil until golden. Serve hot.

VEGETABLE PURÉES

These are the purest of sauces. Made almost entirely from a single cooked vegetable, each purée is full-flavored and a brilliant color. Use vegetable purées in any variety of ways. (Suggestions are included with each recipe.) You'll be amazed by how good such simplicity can be!

❁ RED PEPPER PURÉE ❁

2 large red bell peppers
¼ tsp. salt
A pinch of sugar

½ tsp. fresh lemon juice
1 scant tsp. minced garlic
Black pepper, to taste

1) Core the peppers and cut them into large chunks.
2) Steam over boiling water for about 10 minutes, or until very soft.
3) Purée in a food processor or blender, and pass through a mesh strainer into a bowl. Stir in remaining ingredients, adjusting amounts to taste.

→ Spoon room-temperature sauce over Stuffed Eggplant (p. 151) or Zuccanoes (p. 154). OTHER USES: In or on omelettes; on fish, baked potatoes, or other cooked vegetables; as a garnish on soup — or just spread on toast.

NOTE: You can roast the peppers instead of steaming them. Just put them on an oiled tray in a 400°F oven, and roast until very tender (about 20 to 30 minutes). Transfer with tongs to a glass or ceramic bowl, cover it with a plate, and let sit for 30 minutes longer. Remove skins, stems, and seeds, and proceed with Step 3 above.

✿ BEET PURÉE ✿

2 beets (2½-inch diameter)
½ cup apple or orange juice
2 Tbs. fresh lemon juice
1 Tbs. cider vinegar

2 tsp. honey
½ tsp. salt
Black pepper, to taste
Minced fresh tarragon or mint (optional)

1) Cook the beets until tender. (You can boil them, or roast them on an oiled tray in a 400°F oven.) Cool until comfortable to handle.
2) Rub off the skins, rough-chop the beets, and put them in a blender or food processor with the fruit juices and vinegar. Purée until smooth.

3) Transfer to a small bowl, and stir in honey, salt, pepper, and possibly the tarragon or mint. If necessary, thin to desired consistency with a little extra apple or orange juice.

→ Serve room-temperature sauce over hardboiled eggs, Kristina's Potato Salad (p. 52), Zuccanoes (p. 154), or Stuffed Squash (p.152).

❀ CARROT PURÉE ❀

A little oil for the baking tray
3 medium carrots, peeled and cut into 1-inch chunks OR
1 pound baby carrots

A scant ½ tsp. salt

¼ tsp. cumin (optional)
¼ tsp. minced garlic
1 tsp. minced fresh dill
3 Tbs. orange juice (maybe more)
½ tsp. fresh lemon juice
1 cup water

1) Preheat oven to 400°F. Lightly oil a baking tray, and spread out the carrots. Roast for 20 to 30 minutes, or until tender. Remove from oven, and allow the carrots to cool for about 15 minutes.

2) Put the cooked carrots in a food processor or blender with all the other ingredients, and purée until very smooth. (You may need to do this in batches.) For an even silkier result, pour the purée through a mesh strainer into a bowl.

3) Correct seasonings, if necessary. If you'd like, you could thin the purée a little by adding a small amount of extra orange juice.

→ Serve room-temperature purée on cooked asparagus or broccoli; as a garnish on soup; on Crêpes (p. 142), Zuccanoes (p. 154), baked or grilled fish, or on whatever else you can think of.

❀ SPINACH PURÉE ❀

1 lb. fresh spinach, stemmed and cleaned

¼ to ½ cup water
¼ to ½ tsp. salt

1 medium clove garlic, minced
black pepper, to taste

1) Cook the spinach without added water in a covered pot for just a few minutes — until tender and very bright green.

2) Transfer to a blender or food processor, and add ¼ cup water. Purée until very smooth, and place in a small bowl. Thin to desired consistency with a little more water (or leave it thick). Season to taste with salt, garlic, and black pepper. Serve on cold steamed vegetables, on hot baked potatoes, on baked fish, on cold pasta...etc.

Basic Stir-Fry Sauce

Preparation time:
10 minutes

Yield: enough for
6 servings

Designed to enhance Chinese-Style Stir-Fried Vegetables (recipe follows), this sauce is gingery, garlicky, and thickened just enough to give each vegetable a delicious, deeply flavored coating. You can also use this sauce (minus the cornstarch) for baked fish, or as a dipping sauce for Chinese Green Onion Pancakes (p. 115).

¼ cup soy sauce
1¼ cups water
1 Tbs. grated ginger
2 large cloves garlic, minced

1 tsp. sesame oil
1 Tbs. sugar
1 Tbs. plus 1 tsp. cider vinegar
2 Tbs. dry sherry or Chinese rice wine

3 Tbs. cornstarch

1) Combine all ingredients except cornstarch in a small bowl or a 2-to 4-cup liquid measuring cup.
2) Place the cornstarch in a separate small bowl, and whisk in the mixture from Step 1.

Chinese-Style Stir-Fried Vegetables

Preparation time:
20 minutes for chopping;
15 minutes to stir-fry

Yield: 4 to 6
servings

There is no one correct method for stir-frying vegetables, and many of us already have our own individual (if not idiosyncratic) style. But just in case you are new to this, here is a basic method. (If you would like a more detailed description, including methods for cutting various vegetables, there is an 8-page section on sautéed vegetable dinners in the sequel to this book, The Enchanted Broccoli Forest.)

NOTE: Cook the rice or noodles first. Begin the rice at least 30 minutes before you start the stir-fry. (For 6 servings: 2½ cups raw brown rice in 3¼ cups boiling water, covered, for about 40 minutes over lowest heat.) If you are using noodles, cook them just before you start the stir-fry. Use about ¾ lb. (raw measure) vermicelli or flat egg noodles. Drain the cooked noodles, drizzle with a little sesame oil, and, if desired, keep them warm in a 200°F. oven.

Here is a sample assortment of vegetables that will feed 4 to 6 people. Remember, the amounts are approximate, and the vegetables themselves are flexible. Use whatever is in season. Harder, firmer vegetables (carrots, broccoli, etc.) take longer to cook and should go into the wok earlier. Medium-soft vegetables (mushrooms, zucchini, etc.) go in midway through the cooking. Very soft vegetables (leafy greens, etc.) go in last.

Have the sauce prepared and all the vegetables cut and at hand before beginning. The stir-fry goes quickly, and you don't want to overcook anything.

2 to 3 Tbs. peanut oil
1 medium-sized (3-inch diameter) onion, chopped
½ tsp. salt
a 1½-lb. bunch broccoli, cut into 3-inch spears
1 medium (7-inch diameter) head cauliflower, broken or chopped into 1-inch florets
1 large carrot, in thin slices
4 cups coarsely chopped cabbage

½ lb. mushrooms, sliced
1 medium (7-inch) zucchini, quartered lengthwise and cut into 1-inch pieces
a few handfuls fresh spinach
1 batch Basic Stir-Fry Sauce (preceding page) or a double batch of Orange-Ginger Sauce (next page)

cooked rice or noodles

1) Heat a large (12-inch diameter or more) wok or a deep skillet for about 1 minute over medium heat.
2) Add oil, onion, and salt. Stir-fry for about a minute.
3) Add broccoli, cauliflower, carrot, and cabbage, and turn up the heat. Stir-fry for about 3 or 4 minutes, or until the vegetables begin to get tender.
4) Add mushrooms and zucchini. Stir-fry another 4 or 5 minutes, or until the zucchini begins to get soft. Add spinach.
5) Whisk the sauce from the bottom to reincorporate the cornstarch, and pour all of it in. Stir from the bottom of the wok or skillet, and keep the heat constantly high. Within about 3 minutes the sauce will thicken and turn all the vegetables shiny.
6) Remove from heat, spoon over rice or noodles, and serve right away.

Orange-Ginger Sauce

Serve on stir-fried vegetables (see preceding pages), on vegetable-filled Crêpes (p. 143), on plain cooked rice, on fish or chicken, or on Stuffed Squash (p. 152-3).

2 Tbs. cornstarch
1 cup orange juice
2 to 3 medium cloves garlic, minced
1 Tbs. minced fresh ginger
¼ cup soy sauce

salt, pepper, and cayenne, to taste
OPTIONAL ADDITIONS:
½ tsp. grated orange rind
1 to 2 Tbs. honey
1 to 2 Tbs. dry sherry
1 scallion, finely minced

1) Place cornstarch in a small bowl (if you're using this for stir-fried vegetables) or in a small saucepan (if you're using this for anything else).
2) Add orange juice, and whisk until the cornstarch dissolves. Stir in all remaining ingredients (including optional additions).
3) If you are using the sauce for stir-fried vegetables, stir from the bottom, and add to the wok or skillet about midway through the cooking (see detailed instructions on the previous 2 pages). If you are using this for anything else, place the saucepan over medium heat, and gradually bring to a boil, whisking constantly. Lower heat to a simmer and cook, whisking frequently, until thick and glossy (3 to 5 minutes). Serve hot or warm.

Cashew-Ginger Sauce

Use this quick & easy sauce on plain cooked rice, steamed broccoli, or baked eggplant slices. It's also a good accompaniment to curries (p. 172-5) and Stuffed Cabbage (p. 155).

2 cups toasted cashews
1 cup water
2 Tbs. minced fresh ginger
1 Tbs. soy sauce

1 Tbs. honey or sugar (white or brown)
2 Tbs. plus 1 tsp. cider vinegar
½ tsp. salt
cayenne, to taste

Purée everything together in a food processor or blender. When it is as smooth as you like it, transfer to a tightly lidded container and refrigerate. Heat gently before serving.

TOFU-BASED SAUCES

♥ ♥

In my search for ways to make sauces without dairy products, I was thrilled to discover something called silken tofu. It is the smoothest edible substance imaginable — and utterly neutral in flavor. Whether it is labeled "soft", "firm", or "extra firm", silken tofu has enough body to be whipped easily into a state resembling thick mayonnaise — and to hold this form, if stored properly, for days.

Here are 4 very simple sauces, made in less than 5 minutes each.

NOTE: Silken tofu comes in little vacuum-packed boxes, and is sold in most natural foods stores. Because of the ingenious way in which it is packaged, it has a long shelf life before it is opened.

♥ ♥

For each of the following, use <u>1 box (10 ½ oz.) silken tofu</u>, soft or firm. Place all ingredients in a blender, and whip until smooth. Store in a tightly covered container in the refrigerator. Serve cold or at room temperature. Each is good for sandwiches, baked potatoes, steamed vegetable topping, artichoke dipping, and anywhere you would use mayonnaise.

I. Plain Fake Mayo
1 small clove garlic, minced
2 to 3 tsp. cider vinegar
½ tsp. salt

▸ ▸ ▸ ▸

II. Faux Aioli
2 to 3 medium cloves garlic, minced
½ tsp. salt
½ tsp. dry mustard
½ tsp. cider vinegar
OPTIONAL: a small handful of freshly minced chives and/or parsley.

III. Greek Lemon Sauce
(NOTE: In earlier editions, this was made with an egg plus an extra yolk. No more!)
1 Tbs. fresh lemon juice
½ tsp. salt
a few dashes of white pepper

◂ ◂ ◂ ◂

IV. Horseradish Sauce
(Formerly, this contained sour cream and egg yolks. Unnecessary!)
2 tsp. fresh lemon juice
½ tsp. salt
2 tsp. prepared horseradish
white pepper, to taste
OPTIONAL: minced chives

♥ ♥ ♥ ♥ ♥ ♥ ♥ ♥ ♥ ♥ ♥

Preparation time:
20 minutes

Yield: 4 to 5
servings

Here is your regular old-fashioned cheese sauce, spruced up a little. Whip this up whenever you need some comfort food in a hurry. Serve it in or over omelettes, over steamed vegetables (especially cauliflower, broccoli, or asparagus), or even over whole wheat toast with some sliced apples on top. And when you feel tugs of longing and nostalgia, you can mother yourself by mixing Zippy Cheese Sauce with cooked macaroni (use 3/4 lb. raw macaroni with a batch of this sauce for 3 to 4 servings) and some extra cheese. Bake it in a casserole with bread crumbs on top at 350°F until heated through (about 30 minutes) for 1950s-style Macaroni and Cheese.

2 Tbs. butter
2 Tbs. flour
1 Tbs. dry mustard
2 cups warm milk (lowfat OK)
1 cup (packed) grated cheese (a medium-sharp
        cheddar works well)
salt and white pepper, to taste
OPTIONAL ADDITIONS:
        1 to 2 tsp. prepared horseradish
        a few shakes Tabasco Sauce
        1 small clove garlic, minced

1) Melt the butter over low heat in a small saucepan.

2) Whisk in the flour and dry mustard; keep whisking for about a minute after it dissolves.

3) Add the milk. Cook over medium heat, whisking frequently, for about 5 minutes, or until thickened.

4) Add the cheese, and stir until it melts.

5) Season to taste with salt, white pepper, and optional hot stuff.

Rarebit

... the old-fashioned Welsh cheese sauce, spiked with beer. Serve this over toast and/or steamed broccoli or asparagus. This also works beautifully as a sauce for baked or boiled potatoes.

2 Tbs. butter
2 Tbs. flour
1 tsp. dry mustard
1½ cups beer or ale, at room temperature
      (ok if flat)
1 packed cup grated cheddar (about ½ lb.)
1 tsp. prepared horseradish
1 medium clove garlic, minced
salt, black pepper, and cayenne — to taste

UNDERNEATH THE SAUCE:
toast, and/or
steamed broccoli or asparagus, and/or
baked or boiled potatoes

NEXT TO, OR ON TOP OF, THE SAUCE:
chunks of ripe tomato
slices of tart apple
chopped, toasted walnuts

1) Melt the butter in a medium-sized saucepan. Sprinkle in the flour and dry mustard, whisking constantly.

2) Add the beer or ale, and keep whisking as you bring it to a boil. Lower the heat, and simmer for about 10 minutes, mixing frequently.

3) Add the remaining ingredients, and stir until the cheese melts. Serve hot over thick slices of toast (sourdough, rye, or pumpernickel are especially good) or over steamed vegetables and/or cooked potatoes. Garnish with tomatoes or apples, and if it appeals to you, a few toasted walnuts.

Nachos Sauce

Watch this sauce turn plain beans, rice, and tortillas into a special meal. Serve with a green salad topped with Guacamole (p. 108).

TO PEEL AND SEED THE TOMATOES: Cut out the cores, and immerse the tomatoes in simmering water for a slow count of 10. Retrieve the tomatoes, peel them, and cut them open. Squeeze out and discard the seeds; chop the remaining pulp.

2 Tbs. olive oil
1½ cups chopped onion
¾ tsp. salt
1 tsp. cumin
½ tsp. coriander
¼ tsp. cayenne
1 large bell pepper, diced
3 medium-sized ripe tomatoes, peeled, seeded, and chopped (see above)
2 Tbs. flour
12 oz. beer or ale (not too bitter) (OK if flat), at room temperature
3 medium cloves garlic, minced
1 to 2 tsp. sugar, if necessary (if the beer is still too bitter in spite of your best intentions)
2 cups (packed) mild white cheese (can be reduced or omitted)
optional: freshly minced cilantro, for the top

1) Heat olive oil in a medium-sized saucepan. Add onion and salt, and sauté for 5 minutes, or until the onion is soft.
2) Add cumin, coriander, cayenne, bell pepper, and tomatoes. Cover and cook over medium heat, stirring occasionally, for about 30 minutes. The peppers should be very tender.
3) Whisk in the flour, making sure all the lumps dissolve. Stir in the beer, bring to a boil, then lower heat to a simmer. Cook gently, uncovered for about 15 minutes. Stir in the garlic; cook 5 minutes more. Taste, and add sugar, if needed.
4) Add the cheese, stirring until it melts. Serve hot over beans and rice (or cooked vegetables or whatever) with freshly steamed tortillas. Sprinkle freshly minced cilantro over the top.

MEXICAN RED SAUCE

Preparation time:
about 30 minutes
mostly for simmering

Yield: enough for
6 servings of
Enchiladas (p. 167)
and 8 servings
of Tostadas (p. 168)

2 tsp. olive oil
1 cup minced onion
½ tsp. salt
1½ tsp. cumin
2 tsp. chili powder
3 cups chopped tomatoes (4 to 6 medium-sized ones) - peeling
    and seeding optional (see instructions on opposite page)
1 cup water or tomato juice
black pepper and cayenne, to taste
4 to 6 medium cloves garlic, minced
optional: freshly minced cilantro, for the top

1) Heat olive oil in a medium-sized saucepan. Add onion and salt, and sauté over medium heat for about 5 minutes, or until the onion is translucent. Add cumin and chili powder, and sauté about 5 minutes more.

2) Add chopped tomatoes and water or juice. Bring to a boil, partially cover, and lower heat. Simmer at least 30 minutes (or even longer). Add the black pepper, cayenne, and garlic at any time during the cooking. (The later you add the garlic, the more distinct its presence.) Add the cilantro when you are finished cooking the sauce.

3) The sauce can be left in chunky form, or you can purée all or part of it in a blender or food processor.

HOT SAUCE VARIATION:

Follow the recipe for Mexican Red Sauce. When you sauté the onion, add 1 Tbs. or more crushed red pepper or 1 to 2 tsp. finely minced serrano or jalapeño chilies. (Be very careful to wash your hands thoroughly after handling any part of the chilies, or even after thinking about them.)

SALSA FRESCA

Great as a dip for chips, with any bean dish, next to omelettes, with plain rice, on top of Tostadas (p. 168-9), or in partnership with Zingy Bean Dip (p. 106) or Guacamole (p. 108). If you eat chicken or fish, try serving the Pineapple or Mango Salsa alongside — they make exquisite relishes.

Pineapple Salsa

2 cups minced fresh (or canned-in-juice) pineapple
2 medium cloves garlic, minced
2 to 3 Tbs. minced fresh mint
2 Tbs. fresh lime juice
¼ tsp. salt
¼ tsp. cumin
cayenne, to taste

15 minutes to prepare (w/ fresh pineapple) OR 5 minutes (w/ canned) — Yield: 2 cups

Combine everything, cover tightly, and refrigerate. This keeps a long time.

For an exotic taste sensation, try spooning a little of this onto a bowlful of Brazilian Black Bean Soup (p. 26).

Mango Salsa

2 Tbs. finely minced red onion
2 cups boiling water
1 average-sized (about 6 inches long) ripe mango (if you're lucky enough to find one) — about 1½ cups minced
2 Tbs. fresh lime juice
1 medium clove garlic, minced
½ tsp. salt
2 Tbs. minced fresh cilantro
optional: cayenne, to taste

10 minutes to prepare
Yield: 1½ cups

Place the minced onion in a small strainer over a bowl. Slowly pour the boiling water over the onion, then let it sit for 5 minutes. This will soften its bite, and turn it a striking shade of purple-pink.
Combine all ingredients and mix gently. Cover tightly and refrigerate.

Tomato Salsa

3 medium-sized ripe tomatoes
2 scallions, finely minced
2 medium cloves garlic, minced
a handful of parsley, finely minced
a handful of cilantro, finely minced
1 tsp. lightly toasted cumin seeds
¾ to 1 tsp. salt
1 Tbs. cider vinegar
1 Tbs. olive oil
1 Tbs. fresh lime juice
crushed red pepper, to taste

10 minutes to prepare
Yield: 1½ to 2 cups

Drop the tomatoes into a potful of simmering water for 10 seconds. Take them out, pull off the skins, and squeeze out the seeds. Dice the remaining pulp. Combine everything in a small bowl or container. Cover tightly and chill.

NOTE: To toast the cumin seeds, use a small skillet over a low flame or a toaster oven. With either method, watch them carefully so they won't scorch.

Preparation time:
10 minutes
to assemble;
30 minutes
to simmer

Yield:
about 2 cups

You can buy duck or plum sauce in most Asian groceries, but homemade is easy — and distinctly better. Keep this around to use as a condiment for many different things. You can mix Eastern metaphors by serving this alongside Thai Salad (p. 50) or Indonesian Rice Salad (p. 51), or with Samosas (p. 170). Duck Sauce is also good with squash casseroles (p. 140) or Stuffed Squash (p. 152).

This keeps very well for weeks if stored in a sterile airtight container in the refrigerator.

> 5 cups mixed peeled, chopped fruit (apples, pears, peaches, and/or plums)
> 1 cup water
> ¼ cup cider vinegar
> ¼ cup (packed) light brown sugar
> ¼ tsp. salt
> 2 to 3 medium cloves garlic, minced
> ½ tsp. dry mustard
> optional: up to ½ tsp. crushed red pepper

1) Combine everything in a medium-sized saucepan and bring to a boil.

2) Turn the heat down, and simmer uncovered until all the fruit is very soft (about 30 minutes).

3) Cool thoroughly, then chill.

CHUTNEY

Serve chutney with any Indian dish (see pages 170 through 175), and with whatever else you can think of: sandwiches (see p. 117, and pages 120-21), soups, stews, and if you are not a vegetarian, with fish or chicken.

These 2 chutneys are easy to make. Just combine everything in a saucepan, bring it to a boil, and let it simmer. It's hard to go wrong. <u>Preparation time for each</u>: a few minutes to assemble, plus 45 minutes to cook. Then cool and chill. <u>Yield</u>: about 1½ cups each. Chutney keeps very well in the refrigerator if kept in a sterile, tightly lidded jar — and it goes a long way.

APPLE CHUTNEY

1½ lbs. tart apples
1 medium clove garlic, minced
1 Tbs. minced fresh ginger
1 tsp. cinnamon
1 tsp. cloves or allspice
½ tsp. salt
½ cup (packed) brown sugar
⅓ cup cider vinegar
cayenne, to taste

1) Coarsely chop the apples (peeling is optional). Place them in a medium-sized saucepan with all remaining ingredients. Bring to a boil, then lower heat to a simmer.
2) Simmer uncovered for about 45 minutes, or until everything is very soft. Cool, then transfer to a sterile jar with a lid. Chill.

TOMATO CHUTNEY

2 lbs. unripe tomatoes (about 6 medium-sized ones, the greener, the better)
2 Tbs. minced fresh ginger
1 tsp. mustard seeds
1 tsp. cumin seeds

1 tsp. coriander (optional)
¾ tsp. salt
¼ cup cider vinegar
¼ cup (packed) brown sugar
¼ cup white sugar
cayenne, to taste
2 Tbs. minced garlic

1) Dice the tomatoes, and place them in a medium-sized saucepan with all remaining ingredients, except the garlic.
2) Bring to a boil, lower the heat, and simmer uncovered for 45 minutes or until everything is well mingled and very soft. Add the garlic during the last 5 or 10 minutes of cooking. Cool, then transfer to a sterile jar with a lid, and chill.

RAITA

One of the many condiments served in a traditional Indian meal, Raita is a yogurt preparation with small amounts of seasoning and a hint of minced or grated fresh vegetables. It is designed to cool and relax the palate between bites of heavier, more intensely seasoned dishes. Serve Raita with any curry (see pages 172 through 175) or with Samosas (p. 170) or with Gingered Carrot Soup (p. 22) or Curried Squash and Mushroom Soup (p. 15). This can be put together in just minutes.

NOTE: For a deeper flavor, the cumin and optional fennel seeds can be lightly toasted first. Cook them without oil in a small, heavy skillet over medium heat, stirring frequently, for about a minute — or until they give off a toasty aroma.

2 cups yogurt

1 tsp. cumin seeds

salt and cayenne, to taste

OPTIONAL ADDITIONS (add some or all):

1 small cucumber (about 5 inches long), peeled, seeded, and minced or grated

1 small ripe tomato, diced

¼ cup finely minced onion

½ cup finely minced bell pepper (any color)

½ tsp. fennel seeds

Combine everything in a small bowl and mix gently. Cover tightly, and refrigerate until serving time.

10 minutes to prepare
(after chick peas are
cooked)

HUMMUS

A tangy and delicious chick pea purée from the Middle East, Hummus is a perfect dip or sandwich spread, and an ideal component for a Mezza (see below). Preparation is super-quick if you use a food processor.

NOTE: This recipe calls for 3 cups cooked chick peas. You can soak and cook dry ones, but canned work just as well.

2 to 3 medium cloves garlic, sliced
a large handful of parsley
2 healthy scallions, in 1-inch pieces
3 cups cooked chick peas (two 15½-oz.
   cans, rinsed and well drained)

6 Tbs. tahini
6 Tbs. fresh lemon juice
¾ to 1 tsp. salt (to taste)
optional: cayenne and a little
   cumin, to taste

1) Place garlic, parsley, and scallions in a food processor or blender, and mince
2) Add chick peas, tahini, lemon juice, and salt, and purée to a thick paste. (You can also do the mincing and mashing by hand. The Hummus will have a coarser texture, but that can be nice, too.)
3) Season to taste, if desired, with cayenne and cumin (and correct the salt, if necessary). Transfer to a tightly lidded container and chill.

MEZZA

In Middle Eastern and some Balkan cuisines, it is common to serve a variety of appetizers, dips, salads, and garnishes on a platter (or several platters) at the beginning of a festive meal — or as the meal itself. Here is a list of the dishes in this book that could be used in any combination to make a Mezza at home for your family and friends. Don't forget to garnish lavishly — make it beautiful! Serve with Pita Bread (p. 113) and/or sesame crackers.

Tabouli (p. 46)
Lentil-Bulgur Salad (p. 47)
Eggplant Dips (p. 104-5)
Hummus (above)

Tahini-Lemon Sauce (p. 103)
Yogurt Cheese (p. 102)
Wicked Garlic Dip (p. 102)
Walnut Pâtés (opposite page)

Felafel (p. 116)
Balkan Cucumber
   Salad (p. 69)
Stuffed Grape Leaves
   (p. 149)

Garnishes: ☆ small sprigs of fresh herbs (parsley, mint, thyme, marjoram, dill, cilantro) ☆ pepperoncini ☆ Kalamata olives ☆ radishes, plus small, artful cuts of other vegetables ☆ feta cheese ☆ cherry tomatoes ☆ beautiful red pomegranate seeds sprinkled over the top of everything

Two Exotic Walnut Pâtés

Feta-Walnut Dip

10 minutes to prepare
Yield: about 6 servings

1 cup chopped walnuts
a handful of fresh parsley
1 cup crumbled feta cheese
½ cup water or milk
optional: 1 small clove of garlic

1 tsp. paprika
cayenne, to taste
a little olive oil
a little oregano (dried, or even
    better: a few fresh sprigs)

1) Place the walnuts and parsley in a blender or food processor, and blend with a series of quick spurts.
2) When the nuts are ground, add remaining ingredients except olive oil and oregano, and purée until smooth.
3) Transfer to a small serving bowl, cover tightly, and chill. Just before serving, drizzle the top with a little olive oil, and garnish with small sprigs of fresh (or a light sprinkling of dried) oregano. Serve on sesame crackers or toasted pita wedges, or as a dip for raw vegetables.

Vegetable-Walnut Pâté

30 minutes to prepare
Yield: about 6 servings

It really does taste like chopped liver.

1 Tbs. vegetable oil
½ cup minced onion
½ tsp. salt
1½ cups chopped fresh green beans
2 hardboiled eggs (yolks may
    be omitted)

¼ cup chopped walnuts
1 to 2 Tbs. white wine — or
    2 tsp. fresh lemon juice
1 to 2 Tbs. Mayonnaise (p.44)
black pepper, to taste
a handful of parsley

1) Heat oil in a small skillet. Add onion and salt, and sauté over medium heat for about 10 minutes — until the onion begins to brown. Add the green beans, and sauté until they are tender (another 8 to 10 minutes).
2) Combine everything in a blender or food processor and grind into a uniform paste. (You can also chop or mash it by hand, à la countless grandmothers.) Serve as an appetizer with crackers and raw vegetables, or as a great sandwich spread.

Yogurt Cheese

Yogurt can be made into a lovely soft cheese by simply pressing out much of its water. You can use lowfat or even nonfat yogurt, and still, the resulting cheese will be thick and rich tasting.

The procedure:

1) Start with double the amount you want to end up with. So, in order to get 1 cup of yogurt cheese, use 2 cups of yogurt. Place a colander in the sink, and line it with about 6 layers of cheesecloth, cut to about 10 inches.
2) Place the yogurt in the cheesecloth, wrap the cloth around it, and secure it tightly with a clip or a bag tie.
3) Place a 2- to 3-lb. bag of beans on top, and let it sit there for at least 6 to 8 hours. The water from the yogurt will slowly drip out the bottom, and the creamy solids will remain. (NOTE: The longer it sits, weighted and dripping, the thicker the cheese will be.)
4) Remove the cheesecloth, wrap the cheese well, and refrigerate. To serve, top with a drizzle of olive oil and small amounts of freshly minced herbs (marjoram, dill, parsley, chives), or just a little salt and some freshly ground pepper. Serve as an appetizer (see Mezza, p. 100) or keep on hand for sandwiches.

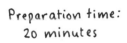

Preparation time: 20 minutes

Wicked Garlic Dip

Yield: about 2 cups (a little goes a long way)

3 medium (average fist-sized) potatoes, peeled and diced
3 medium cloves garlic, peeled
up to 1/3 cup mayonnaise (see p. 44 and p. 91)
1/2 tsp. salt

1) Boil the potatoes until very soft, and drain well. Transfer to a food processor fitted with the steel blade, or to a mixing bowl.
2) Without waiting for the potatoes to cool, add the remaining ingredients. Whip until very smooth, using either the food processor or an electric mixer.
3) Cover tightly and chill. Serve as an appetizer (see Mezza, p. 100) or by itself, garnished with raw vegetables, or as a spread (great on sesame crackers or toasted pita wedges).

Tahini-Lemon Sauce

Make a batch of this on a regular basis—it's remarkably quick and easy. It can be thinned down to the consistency of a salad dressing (try it on romaine lettuce with chunks of ripe tomato and Kalamata olives) or left thick enough to be either a spread or a dip for raw vegetables and crackers. Find a consistency somewhere between thick and thin, and use it as a sauce for steamed greens, carrots, and cauliflower. Serve it with Felafel (p. 116), or drizzled over Hummus (p.100) in a pita bread (p. 113) sandwich. Tahini-Lemon Sauce is as indispensable as it is hard to categorize. By the way, another attribute: it keeps for weeks if stored in the refrigerator in an airtight container.

3/4 cup sesame tahini
5 Tbs. fresh lemon juice
1 small to medium clove garlic, minced
3/4 to 1½ cups water (depending on desired thickness)
½ to 1 tsp. salt, to taste (will vary with amount of water used)
a handful of very finely minced fresh parsley
optional: cayenne, to taste

1) Place tahini, lemon juice, and garlic in a food processor fitted with the steel blade. (You can also use a blender.) Begin to process.
2) Keeping the motor running, slowly drizzle in the water, checking every now and then to monitor the consistency. When it is as thick/thin as you want it, turn off the machine.
3) Transfer to a small bowl or container, and season to taste with salt, parsley, and, if desired, cayenne. Cover tightly and refrigerate until ready for use.

EGGPLANT DIPS

Baba Ganouj

The classic Middle Eastern eggplant appetizer, plus a few variations on the theme. The instructions call for baking the eggplant, but if you have the opportunity to grill it over hot coals or to roast it over a direct flame, the Baba Ganouj will taste even better.

40 minutes to prepare

a little oil, for the baking sheet
1 medium (1-inch) eggplant
2 medium cloves garlic, minced
¼ cup fresh lemon juice
¼ cup sesame tahini
½ tsp. salt
black pepper and cayenne, to taste
olive oil } for the top
freshly minced parsley }

Yield: 4 to 6 servings

1) Preheat oven to 350°F. Lightly oil a baking sheet.
2) Slice the eggplant in half lengthwise, and place face-down on the baking sheet. Bake for 30 minutes or until very tender. Cool until it's comfortable to handle.
3) Scoop out the eggplant pulp, and discard the skin. Place the pulp in a food processor or blender, and add the garlic, lemon juice, tahini, and salt. Purée until smooth. (Another alternative is to mash by hand, leaving the eggplant a little chunky.)
4) Transfer to an attractive serving dish, cover tightly, and chill. Drizzle the top with a little olive oil and sprinkle with minced parsley just before serving. Serve with crackers. (Also, see Mezza, p.100.)

VARIATIONS:

I.   1 Tbs. olive oil
     1 cup finely minced onion
     ½ lb. mushrooms, minced   Heat olive oil in a small skillet. Add every-
     ½ tsp. salt   thing else and sauté 10 to 15 minutes,
     1 tsp. dill   or until tender. Stir into puréed eggplant
                                mixture.

II. ½ cup firm yogurt or Greek Lemon Sauce (p. 91)   Add to purée;
     ½ tsp. cumin   mix well.

Spicy Eggplant Relish

Serve this as an accompaniment to any curry (p. 172-75), with Samosas (p. 170), Hummus (p. 100), Felafel (p. 116), or Tabouli (p. 46). It is also good on plain crackers or as a dip for raw vegetables.

    2 Tbs. olive oil
    1 cup minced onion
    1 medium eggplant (7 to 8 inches long), diced
    ½ tsp. salt
    ½ tsp cumin
    1 medium-sized bell pepper, minced
    1 medium clove garlic, minced
    1 Tbs. lemon juice
    cayenne, to taste

1) Heat olive oil in a medium-sized skillet. Add onion, eggplant, salt, and cumin, and sauté over medium heat for 15 to 20 minutes — until the eggplant is tender.

2) Add bell pepper, and sauté for about 10 minutes more.

3) Stir in garlic and lemon juice. Cook for about 5 more minutes. Add cayenne to taste, and adjust the salt, if necessary. You can leave it chunky, or mash a little bit by hand. Serve warm, at room temperature, or cold.

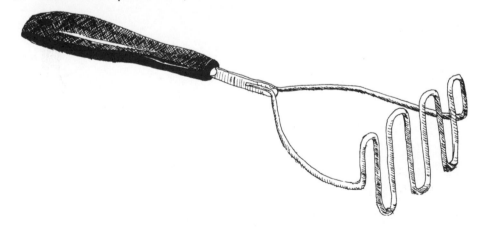

Zingy Bean Dip

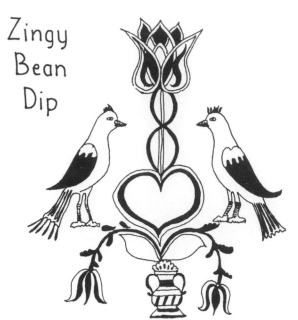

Preparation time:
less than 10
minutes

Yield: about
2 cups

It's hard to find anything new to say in the Bean Dip Department, but this one gets a few words in.

Canned pinto beans work so well in here that I encourage you to use them. Be sure to rinse and drain them well. If you also use a food processor, this recipe will be very quick.

Serve it with chips, vegetables, crackers, or warmed flour tortillas. Pair it with any Salsa Fresca (p. 96) for some serious appetizer activity.

To peel and seed a tomato: Drop it into a pan of boiling water for 10 seconds. Remove it, and peel off the skin. Cut the tomato open; squeeze out and discard the seeds. Chop the remaining pulp.

2 cups cooked pinto beans (one 15-oz. can),
       rinsed and well drained
2 Tbs. fresh lime juice
1 medium-sized tomato, peeled and seeded (see above)
1 to 2 medium cloves garlic, minced
a handful of parsley
a handful of cilantro
3/4 tsp. cumin
optional: 1 scallion, minced
1/4 to 1/2 tsp. salt
black pepper and cayenne, to taste

Whip it all up together in a food processor or a blender.

CHINESE PEANUT SAUCE

This sauce is verrrry intense! Try it as a dip for raw and/or lightly steamed vegetables, or as a dressing for cold cooked noodles (you can thin it with a little water for this). You can also use it for Eggplant and Peppers in Spicy Peanut Sauce (below), and serve it as an appetizer.

½ cup good peanut butter
½ cup water
2 Tbs. soy sauce
2 Tbs. sugar
3 medium cloves garlic, minced
1 tsp. cider vinegar
1 to 2 Tbs. minced fresh cilantro
cayenne, to taste
salt, to taste (if peanut butter is unsalted)

1) Place peanut butter in a small bowl. Add the hot water, and stir patiently with a spoon or a small whisk until uniformly mixed.
2) Stir in remaining ingredients and mix well. Cover tightly and refrigerate. Let come to room temperature before serving.

Eggplant & Peppers in Spicy Peanut Sauce

a little oil, for the baking tray
1 medium (7-inch) eggplant, unpeeled, and cut into
    inch-thick strips, then into 2-inch pieces
salt
1 large bell pepper ~ any color, cut into 1-inch pieces
1 recipe Chinese Peanut Sauce (above)

1) Preheat oven to 375°F. Lightly oil a baking tray.
2) Spread the eggplant pieces on the tray and salt lightly. Let stand 10 minutes.
3) Bake the eggplant until tender (about 15 minutes). (Prepare the sauce during this time.) During the last 5 minutes of baking, add the pepper pieces to the tray.
4) Cool the vegetables to room temperature, then transfer to a bowl or container. Add the Chinese Peanut Sauce and mix gently. Serve at room temperature or cold.

Guacamole

For chips and raw vegetables
AND
For Tostadas (p. 168-9)
AND
For Sandwiches
AND
On top of salads
AND
Wherever else you wish to invite it along

BASIC GUACAMOLE:
2 Tbs. fresh lemon or lime juice
2 medium-sized ripe avocadoes
1 to 2 medium cloves garlic, minced
½ tsp. salt (possibly more, to taste)

OPTIONAL AUGMENTATIONS:
½ tsp. cumin (possibly more, to taste)
½ tsp. chili powder
black pepper and cayenne, to taste
tiny amounts of: minced green or red bell pepper
                  peeled, seeded, and finely minced cucumber
                  diced ripe tomato
2 to 3 Tbs. mayonnaise (see p. 44 and p. 91)

1) Place the lemon or lime juice in a medium-sized shallow bowl.

2) Add the avocado (you can just cut it open and spoon it out of its skin), and mash with a fork to whatever consistency you like.

3) Stir in remaining ingredients. Cover tightly and chill. NOTE: To help the Guacamole retain its color, add the avocado pits. Remove them just before serving.

A FEW BAKED THINGS

AND

SANDWICHES

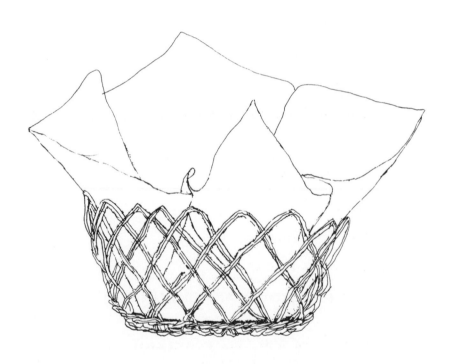

CONTENTS: A FEW BAKED THINGS AND SANDWICHES

CUSTARDY POPOVERS

5 minutes to prepare;
25 to 35 minutes to bake

Yield: 1 dozen

Crisp and puffy, full of hot air and a layer of custard on the inside, Popovers are very easy to throw together on a moment's notice, and they can lend a festive spirit to even a simple bowl of soup. The custard quotient depends on how many eggs you use. This recipe is very flexible, and will work with 2, 3, or 4 eggs.

2 to 3 Tbs. melted butter for the pan
2, 3, or 4 large eggs
1¼ cups milk (lowfat ok)
1¼ cups flour
½ tsp. salt

1) Preheat oven to 375°F. Brush the insides of 12 muffin cups with melted butter.
2) Beat together the eggs and milk in a medium-sized bowl. Add the flour and salt, and beat with a whisk until reasonably well blended. It's fine if the batter has a few lumps.
3) Fill each muffin cup about ½ to ⅔ full. Bake 25 minutes if using 2 eggs, 30 minutes for 3 eggs, and 35 minutes for 4 eggs. Try to refrain from opening the oven during baking.
4) Remove the popovers from the pan immediately, and prick each with a fork to let the steam escape. (This helps them hold their shape.) Serve as soon as possible, either plain or with butter and/or jam.

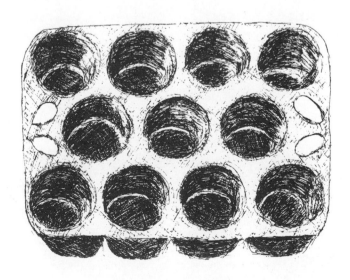

FOCACCIA

~an easy olive oil- and- rosemary- flavored pizza bread. Great with soups, salads, pasta dishes, or chili.

> 1 cup wrist-temperature water
> 1½ tsp. (half a ¼-oz. packet) active dry yeast
> 1 tsp. sugar
> 1 tsp. salt
> approximately 3½ cups flour
> 2 to 3 Tbs. dried rosemary
> olive oil, for the bowl, dough, and baking tray
> extra flour, for handling the dough

1) Follow steps 1, 2, and 3 in the directions for Pita Bread (opposite), adding rosemary with the flour, and using olive oil to oil the dough and the bowl.

2) Punch down the dough, and transfer to a clean floured surface. Adding small amounts of extra flour as needed, to avoid stickiness, knead the dough for about 5 to 8 minutes—until it is smooth and elastic. Form the dough into a ball, and roll it into a 10- to 12-inch diameter circle. Let it rest for about 10 minutes. Meanwhile, preheat the oven to 400°F. Lightly oil a baking tray.

3) Transfer the circle of dough to the baking tray, and brush the top surface of the dough with a little more olive oil. Bake for 20 to 30 minutes, or until lightly browned. (Take it out sooner if you like it softer; later if you like it crisper.) Serve hot, warm, or at room temperature.

Pita Bread
(Arabic Pocket Bread)

Preparation time:
about 2 hours
(most of which
is rising time)

Yield: 6 larger
(or 12 smaller)
pocket breads

1 cup wrist-temperature water

1½ tsp. (half a ¼-oz. packet) active dry yeast

1 Tbs. sugar or honey

1 tsp. salt

about 3½ cups flour (1 cup of it can be whole wheat)

OPTIONAL: 1 Tbs. sesome seeds

a little oil for the dough

extra flour for rolling out

oil or cornmeal, for the baking tray

1) Place the water in a medium-sized bowl and sprinkle in the yeast. Let stand for 5 minutes — it will become foamy.

2) Add sugar or honey and salt. Stir until everything dissolves.

3) Add 3 cups of flour, one cup at a time, mixing enthusiastically with a whisk. As the dough thickens, switch to a wooden spoon and, eventually, your hand. Knead the dough in the bowl for a few minutes, adding up to ½ cup more flour, as needed, to combat stickiness. When the dough is smooth, oil both the bowl and the top surface of the dough. Cover with a clean tea towel, and let rise in a warm place for about an hour, or until the dough has doubled in bulk.

4) Punch down the dough and transfer it to a clean, floured surface. Knead it for about 5 minutes, then divide it into either 6 or 12 equal pieces (depending on what size pitas you want). Knead each little unit for a few minutes, then use a rolling pin to flatten it into a very thin circle. (Make sure there is plenty of flour underneath!) The diameter of each circle is unimportant, as long as it is no thicker than ⅛ inch. Let the circles rest for 30 minutes.

5) Preheat oven to 500°F. Place a baking tray in the oven for a minute or two, to heat it. Then brush it with oil — or dust it with cornmeal. Place as many circles on the tray as will fit without touching, and bake for just 6 to 8 minutes, or until puffed up and very lightly browned.

6) Remove from the oven, and wrap the breads in a clean, slightly damp tea towel, then place in a brown paper bag, closed up, for 15 minutes. This will keep the breads supple. (If you'd prefer the pita bread to be crisp and cracker-like, bake 10 to 12 minutes and simply cool on a rack.)

Basic Corn Bread
plus two tasty variations

10 minutes to assemble
20 minutes to bake

Yield:
1 (8-inch) square
panful

butter, for the pan
1 cup cornmeal
1 cup flour
2 tsp. baking powder
½ tsp. baking soda
½ tsp. salt
1 cup buttermilk or yogurt
1 egg
3 Tbs. sugar or honey
3 Tbs. melted butter or margarine

1) Preheat oven to 350°F. Grease an 8-inch square pan (or a 9- or 10-inch cast-iron skillet) with butter.

2) Combine the dry ingredients in a medium-sized bowl. Combine the wet ingredients (including sugar or honey) separately. Stir the wet mixture into the dry, mixing just enough to thoroughly combine. Spread into the prepared pan.

3) Bake for 20 minutes, or until the center is firm to the touch. Serve hot, warm, or at room temperature.

MEXICAN CORN & CHEESE BREAD

Make the batter as described above, with the following additions:
1 cup fresh or frozen/defrosted corn
½ cup (packed) grated mild white cheese } stir into the
3 to 4 scallions, minced } batter.
OPTIONAL: replace the melted butter with olive oil

BLUEBERRY CORN BREAD

Make the batter as described above, increasing the sugar or honey to ¼ cup. Add 1½ cups fresh blueberries, stirring them gently into the batter. (NOTE: You can also use frozen unsweetened blueberries. Defrost and drain before using.)

FLATBREADS:
FLOUR TORTILLAS, CHAPPATIS, & CHINESE GREEN ONION PANCAKES

Here are three variations on the theme of Flatbread — one Mexican, one Indian, and one Chinese. They are all basically the same — quick and easy, yet somehow exotic beyond the sum of their few simple ingredients.

FLOUR TORTILLAS Serve with soups, salads, bean dishes, or rice.

1 cup flour   ½ cup water   a little oil, for cooking
½ tsp. salt   extra flour, for handling the dough

1) Place the flour and salt in a medium-sized bowl. Add the water, and stir until fairly well combined.

2) Transfer the dough to a clean, floured surface, and knead for a minute or two, adding extra flour, if necessary, to keep it from becoming sticky. Divide the dough into 6 equal balls, and roll each one into a very thin circle — no thicker than ⅛ inch. Use lots of flour, both on the rolling surface and the rolling pin.

3) You can either bake or pan-fry the tortillas. To bake, preheat the oven to 325°F. Place the tortillas on a lightly oiled tray, brush their top surfaces with a little more oil, and bake for 10 to 15 minutes, or until very lightly browned. (Bake them longer if you like them crisper, shorter if you like them softer.) To pan-fry, heat a heavy skillet or a griddle for a few minutes. Add a small amount of oil, and cook the tortillas for 3 to 5 minutes on each side. (Just as with baking, cooking them longer makes them crisper.)

4) Remove the tortillas from the oven, and serve hot or warm. If you need to reheat them, wrap tightly in foil, and place in a 300°F. oven for 10 to 15 minutes.

CHAPPATIS Serve with any soup or with curries (p. 172-75).

Make Flour Tortillas as described above, but substitute ½ cup whole wheat flour for ½ cup of the white flour.

CHINESE GREEN ONION PANCAKES Serve with any soup, with Tofu Salad (p. 56), or with Duck Sauce (p. 97) or Stir-Fry Sauce (p. 88) for an appetizer or snack.

Make Flour Tortillas as described above, adding to the flour mixture: 3 medium-sized scallions, very finely minced. After the pancakes are cooked, sprinkle on a little extra salt.

Felafel

Felafel are small, spicy chick pea patties. They are almost always topped with Tahini-Lemon Sauce (p. 103), and served either in a sandwich with Pita Bread (p. 113), or as an appetizer, either alone, or on a Mezza (p. 100). Traditionally, Felafel are deep-fried, but they are equally good — and satisfyingly crisp — if pan-fried in a very hot skillet with a small amount of oil.

4 cups cooked chick peas (OK to use canned. Two
15-oz. cans will provide the right amount.)

4 medium cloves garlic, minced
2 tsp. cumin
1 tsp. turmeric
1 tsp. salt
½ cup finely minced onion,
  or 6 scallions, minced

¼ cup (packed) minced parsley
¼ cup water
1 Tbs. lemon juice
a few dashes of cayenne
⅓ cup flour
oil for frying

1) Rinse the chick peas, and drain them well.
2) Combine all ingredients except flour in a food processor or a medium-sized bowl and process — or mash — until you have a uniform batter.
3) Add flour, and stir until thoroughly combined. You can cook the Felafel right away, or store the batter in a tightly covered container in the refrigerator for several days.
4) Heat a heavy skillet and add about 3 Tbs. oil. When it is hot enough to sizzle a bread crumb on contact, drop tablespoonfuls of batter into the pan, flattening each slightly, like a small, thick pancake. Sauté for about 10 minutes on each side, until golden and crisp. Add small amounts of extra oil to the pan as needed through-out the cooking.
5) Place the cooked Felafel on a plate lined with paper towels, and, if necessary, keep warm in a 300°F. oven until serving time.

Celebratory Sandwich Fillings

If you pack a lunch for yourself or for members of your family, and you need some inspiration to get away from cheese, egg salad, and peanut butter and jelly, try some of these sandwich filling ideas. Remember that most of them keep for at least several days (and some for longer), so make a few fillings on a weekend, and you'll have inspiration and variety to get you through the week.

1) <u>Eggplant Dips</u>   (p. 104 and 105) go perfectly in Pita Bread (p. 113) or on whole wheat bread.

2) <u>Walnut Pâtés</u> (p. 101) make a substantial sandwich with lettuce and tomato on sourdough or whole wheat bread.

3) Keep <u>Yogurt Cheese</u> (p. 102) on hand. It lasts a long time! You can use it wherever you would cream cheese. Some suggestions: ☆ with toasted cashews and minced candied ginger ☆ with minced fresh herbs (small amounts of parsley, chives, dill, marjoram, thyme, cilantro ~ in any combination) and a few slices of cucumber ☆ with pitted, chopped olives (your favorite kind), minced walnuts, and parsley

4) <u>Tahini-Lemon Sauce</u> (p. 103) – Make it thick; spread it on rye or pumpernickel, with tomato, red onion, cucumber, and possibly some minced bell pepper.

5) <u>Zingy Bean Dip</u> (p. 106) and <u>Hummus</u> (p. 100) make great sandwich fillings on any kind of bread (especially pita). Be sure to include a bag of tortilla chips with this lunch!

6) <u>Guacamole</u> (p. 108) can be a spread as well as a dip. It has a shorter shelf life than all of the above-suggested fillings, so make it no farther in advance than the day before.

7) Instead of peanut butter, try almond or cashew butter, just for variety. Instead of jam or jelly, try actual fresh fruit. The best: slices of tart apple, perfectly ripe peach, or banana. Try inserting some seedless grapes into your nut butter. You may forget you put them there, and at lunchtime you'll get a pleasant surprise.

BLUE CHEESE HEAVEN:
Two Simply Divine Blue Cheese Sandwiches

The ingredient amounts are open-ended in these two sandwich ideas, making them as much suggestions as recipes. This is for flexibility's sake, allowing you to accommodate the number of guests, plus your own tastes and refrigerator contents. ♩Note of encouragement: It's hard to go wrong.

I. SAUTÉED VEGETABLES WITH BLUE CHEESE ON TOAST:

minced garlic
sliced red onion
grated carrot
finely shredded cabbage
grated beets
OPTIONAL: minced broccoli
           minced bell pepper
           sliced mushrooms
a little oil
salt, pepper, and dill —to taste
crumbled blue cheese

Sauté the vegetables in a small amount of oil for about 8 to 10 minutes, or until tender.
Season to taste with salt, pepper, and dill. Stir the crumbled cheese into the hot vegetables.

Take some modest slices of whole wheat, rye, or pumpernickel bread, toast them lightly, and spread them with your choice of: mayonnaise (p. 44), Horseradish Sauce (p. 91), thick yogurt (or Yogurt Cheese - p. 102), or mustard. Spoon the vegetable-cheese filling onto the bread, and serve it open-faced or closed.

II. OPEN-FACED BLUE CHEESE SANDWICH WITH PEARS:

softened cream cheese
cottage cheese
ricotta cheese

Use any of these, or a combination. Lowfat varieties work well.

crumbled blue cheese
finely minced toasted walnuts
whole wheat bread, lightly toasted
slices of fresh pear, sprinkled lightly
    with lemon juice or raspberry vinegar

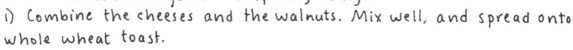

1) Combine the cheeses and the walnuts. Mix well, and spread onto whole wheat toast.
2) Arrange slices of pear on top, and serve.

🍂 Salad 🍂 Sandwiches 🍂

Sometimes that leftover salad — not quite enough to serve again for lunch or even as a side dish for dinner — is really a sandwich filling waiting to happen. Just pile it onto some fresh or toasted bread, close it up, and lunch is ready.

Here are some good candidates for a salad sandwich:

🍂 Warm Salad (p. 40) - Maybe it's room temperature or even cold by now, and it will go beautifully on thick slices of bread or toast.
🍂 March Hare Salad (p. 49)
🍂 Tofu Salad (p. 56) in Pita Bread (p. 113)
🍂 Alsatian Salad (p. 57) — also perfect for Pita
🍂 Marinated Vegetables (p. 63) - on toast, open-faced
🍂 Various Antipasti: Bell Peppers (p. 65), Swiss Chard (p. 66), or Marinated Mushrooms (p. 67) - on toast, open-faced
🍂 Odessa Beets (p. 68) - on rye or pumpernickel, with or without cream cheese

To construct a TOSSED SALAD SANDWICH:
(Seems obvious, but maybe you need permission to leave out the sliced meat or cheese)

- 🍂 slices of great bread
- 🍂 Spread of choice (mayonnaise - p. 44; any dip - p. 100-108)
- 🍂 clean, crisp fresh leafy greens (lettuces, spinach, arugula, herbs)
- 🍂 sliced cucumber
- 🍂 sliced tomato
- 🍂 sliced mushrooms
- 🍂 sliced red onion
- 🍂 grated carrot
- 🍂 slices of avocado
- 🍂 salt and pepper

Broiled and Grilled Sandwiches

Here are some ideas for broiled or grilled sandwiches that can be served for lunch or dinner. You can adjust the amounts and proportions according to your taste, your guests, and what you have on hand. With the exception of Ideas for Cheese, these sandwiches are dairy-free.

IDEAS FOR CHEESE:

☆ Tomato Chutney (p.98) spread on rye, pumpernickel, or whole wheat toast. Place some cheese on top and broil.

☆ Coleslaw (p.72) and/or apple slices on rye, pumpernickel, or whole wheat, with cheese broiled on top.

☆ Chinese Mustard (see below) and/or Horseradish Sauce (p.91) with slices of tomato and Swiss cheese on any kind of bread. Leave open-faced and broil -OR- close up the sandwich and grill on a lightly oiled skillet.

GRILLED PEPPER, ONION, CHINESE MUSTARD & TOFU SANDWICH:

For 4 servings:
a little oil for sautéing
1 small red onion, thinly sliced
1 small bell pepper, in thin strips
salt and pepper, to taste
8 slices whole wheat bread
Chinese Mustard (recipe opposite)
1 cake firm tofu, thinly sliced
a little oil for grilling

CHINESE MUSTARD

2 Tbs. Dijon mustard
2 tsp. Chinese sesame oil
1 tsp. cider vinegar
1 tsp. honey or sugar
optional: a little bit of
  freshly minced cilantro
} Combine

1) Heat a little oil in a small skillet. Add the onion and bell pepper, sprinkle lightly with salt and pepper, and sauté over medium heat until the vegetables are tender (8 to 10 minutes).

2) Lightly toast the bread, and spread each slice with Chinese Mustard. Arrange the sautéed vegetables and slices of tofu on 4 of the slices, and place the remaining mustard-spread bread on top.

3) Grill on a lightly oiled skillet on each side until crisp and brown and heated through. Serve hot.

BROCCOLI & FRIENDS:
For 4 servings:
1 tsp. oil
1 cup thinly sliced onion
3 cups chopped broccoli
salt and pepper, to taste
6 to 8 slices of your favorite bread
Greek Lemon Sauce (p. 91)
freshly minced parsley

1) Heat the oil in a small skillet. Add the onion and broccoli, salt lightly, and sauté over medium heat until tender (8 to 10 minutes). Sprinkle generously with black pepper.
2) Toast the bread, and spread it with a little Greek Lemon Sauce. Spoon on some sautéed broccoli, and top with more sauce.
3) Broil for just a few minutes — until bubbly. Garnish with minced parsley, and serve.

BROILED EGGPLANT WITH FAUX AIOLI & TOMATOES:
For 4 servings:
a little olive oil for the baking tray
1 small eggplant (about 6 inches long), sliced into ¼-inch-thick rounds
6 to 8 slices (depending on their size and shape) sourdough bread
        (or Italian bread)
Faux Aioli (p. 91)
a medium-sized ripe tomato (or 2), sliced
salt and pepper
freshly minced parsley

1) Heat the broiler. Lightly oil a baking tray, and add the eggplant slices. Broil about 10 minutes, or until tender. Remove the tray, but leave the broiler on.
2) Toast the bread, and spread it with Faux Aioli. Add some tomato slices. Layer the broiled eggplant on top, and add salt and pepper. Spoon a little extra Aioli on top, and return to the broiler for just a minute or two — until the sauce is bubbly. Garnish with parsley and serve hot.

Pepper & Onion Shortcake

~ Sautéed peppers and onions in a lightly seasoned yogurt sauce
over warm corn bread

Make a batch of Corn Bread (p. 114) ahead of time. You can warm it in a 300°F. oven while preparing the topping, or toast corn bread chunks or slices just before serving. This makes a perfect lunch on a chilly day, especially when served with Spicy Tomato Soup (p. 4).

1 batch Corn Bread (p. 114)
2 Tbs. olive oil or butter
2 cups thinly sliced onion
½ tsp. salt
3 medium-sized bell peppers (any color), in thin strips
½ tsp. cumin (optional)
black pepper } to taste
cayenne
3 medium cloves garlic, minced
½ cup yogurt (OPTIONAL: add 1 to 2 Tbs. sour cream)
   — at room temperature
freshly minced dill, if available
paprika

1) Heat oil (or melt butter) in a medium-large skillet.
2) Add onion and salt, and sauté over medium-low heat for 10 to 15 minutes, or until the onion is very soft and beginning to brown.
3) Add bell peppers, cumin, black pepper, and cayenne, and continue to sauté until the peppers are tender (about 10 more minutes).
4) Add garlic, and cook just a minute or 2 more. Remove from heat and stir in yogurt (and optional touch of sour cream).
5) Serve immediately, spooned over split chunks of warmed or toasted corn bread and garnished with dill and paprika.

ENTRÉES

CONTENTS : ENTRÉES

✐✐✐ Macaroni & Cheese Lite ✐✐✐
✐✐✐✐✐✐✐✐✐✐✐✐✐

You can improvise by increasing or varying the vegetables. Try modest amounts of chopped cauliflower, broccoli, and/or carrots (always colorful).

½ lb. (approximately 3 cups) dry pasta ~ a short, substantial shape, like fusilli, penne, macaroni, 1-inch shells, etc.

2 Tbs. butter

2 cups chopped onion

2 medium cloves garlic, minced

½ lb. mushrooms, sliced

4 cups shredded cabbage (about ½ an average head)

1 tsp. salt

1 tsp. caraway seeds

1 bunch fresh spinach ~ stemmed and coarsely chopped

1 lb. (2 cups) cottage cheese (can be lowfat)

½ cup buttermilk or yogurt

2 Tbs. fresh (or 2 tsp. dried) dill, finely minced

fresh black pepper, to taste

2 cups (packed) grated cheddar

a handful of sunflower seeds (optional)

1) Preheat oven to 350°F. Lightly grease a 9 x 13-inch baking pan.

2) Cook the pasta until just barely tender. Drain thoroughly, and transfer to a large bowl.

3) Melt the butter in a large, deep skillet, and add the onions. After sautéing for about 5 minutes, add garlic, mushrooms, cabbage, salt, and caraway. Stir, cover, and cook until the cabbage is just tender (10 minutes). Stir in spinach, and remove from heat. Add to the pasta.

4) Stir in cottage cheese, buttermilk, dill, black pepper, and half the cheddar. Taste to adjust seasonings, and spread into the prepared pan. Sprinkle with the remaining cheddar and a few sunflower seeds, and bake uncovered for 20 to 30 minutes, or until heated through.

Broccoli Mushroom Noodle Casserole

30 minutes to prepare; 45 minutes to bake.

Yield: about 6 servings

1 1-lb. (or 12-oz.) package wide flat egg noodles
2 Tbs. butter
2 cups chopped onion
3 medium cloves garlic, minced
1 large bunch fresh broccoli, chopped
1 lb. mushrooms, sliced or chopped
½ tsp. salt (more, to taste)
lots of fresh black pepper
optional: ¼ cup dry white wine
optional: 3 eggs, beaten
3 cups (1½ lbs.) cottage cheese (may be lowfat)
1 cup sour cream (may be lowfat) or buttermilk
1½ cups fine bread crumbs and/or wheat germ
optional: 1 cup (packed) grated medium or sharp cheddar

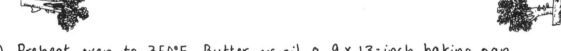

1) Preheat oven to 350°F. Butter or oil a 9 x 13-inch baking pan.

2) Cook the noodles in plenty of boiling water until about half-done. Drain and rinse under cold water. Drain again and set aside.

3) Melt the butter in a large skillet, and add onions and garlic. Sauté for about 5 minutes over medium heat, then add broccoli, mushrooms, salt, and pepper. Continue to cook, stirring frequently, until the broccoli is bright green and just tender. Remove from heat and possibly add optional white wine.

4) In a large bowl, beat together optional eggs (or not) with cottage cheese and sour cream or buttermilk. Add noodles, sautéed vegetables, and 1 cup of the bread crumbs. Mix well.

5) Spread into the prepared pan, and top with remaining bread crumbs and, if desired, grated cheese. Bake covered for 30 minutes; uncovered for 15 minutes more.

noodle kugel

You can make this recipe richer or lighter. Options for both persuasions are listed below.

1 1-lb. (or 12-oz.) package wide egg noodles
2 to 3 Tbs. butter (optional)
3 eggs
2 cups (1 lb.) cottage cheese (lowfat OK)
¾ cup sour cream or yogurt
8 oz. cream cheese (lowfat OK) - optional
1 tsp. vanilla extract
1 to 2 tsp. cinnamon
¼ to ½ cup sugar (to taste)
½ to 1 tsp. salt (to taste)

OPTIONAL ADDITIONS: 1 to 2 Tbs. lemon juice (to taste)
                                ½ cup (packed) raisins
                                1 tart apple, peeled and sliced
                                2 ripe peaches, peeled and sliced

TOPPING (ALSO OPTIONAL): 1 cup bread crumbs and/or wheat germ
                                    1½ tsp. cinnamon
                                    ¼ cup (packed) brown sugar

1) Preheat oven to 375°F. Lightly grease a 9 x 13-inch baking pan.

2) Cook the noodles until about half-done. Drain, and toss with butter (or simply rinse in cold water and drain again). Transfer to a large bowl.

3) Combine eggs, cottage cheese, sour cream or yogurt, cream cheese, cinnamon, sugar, and salt in a blender or food processor and whip until smooth. (Do this in several batches, if necessary.) Stir this into the noodles, along with whatever optional additions you choose. Transfer to the baking pan.

4) Combine the topping ingredients and sprinkle them over the top. Bake uncovered for about 40 minutes. Serve hot, warm, or at room temperature.

I hour to prepare, including baking. (Sauté vegetables while millet cooks.)

Cauliflower Marranca

Yield: 4 to 6 servings

~ a simple cauliflower-mushroom-millet casserole ~

oil for the pan
1½ cups raw millet
2½ cups water
1 Tbs. butter or oil
2 cups chopped onion
1 lb. mushrooms, sliced
black pepper, to taste

1½ tsp. salt
1 tsp. basil
1 large cauliflower, in 1-inch pieces (or smaller)
3 medium cloves garlic, minced
2 to 3 Tbs. lemon juice
OPTIONAL: 1 to 2 cups grated cheese (your choice)
paprika, for the top

PRELIMINARY: Preheat oven to 350°F. Oil a 9x13-inch pan.

1) Place the millet and water in a small saucepan. Bring to a boil, cover, and simmer until tender (15 to 20 minutes). Transfer to a large bowl, and fluff with a fork to let steam escape.

2) Melt butter or heat oil in a large skillet. Add onion, mushrooms, pepper, salt, and basil, and sauté about 5 minutes — until the onions soften. Add cauliflower and garlic, and sauté about 10 minutes more — until the cauliflower is tender. Add lemon juice.

3) Stir the sautéed vegetables into the millet, along with the optional cheese, and mix well. Spread into the prepared pan, dust with paprika, and bake for 30 minutes.

yum yum

Mushroom Moussaka

This is a meatless and eggless version of the famous Greek eggplant casserole, with two deceptively rich-tasting sauces. One is tomato-based and loaded with mushrooms; the other is a traditional Béchamel.

The mushroom sauce can be prepared well ahead of time. You can make the Béchamel while the eggplant slices bake, then assemble the casserole, using the same hot oven for the final baking.

3 medium eggplants (about 7 inches long), peeled or not, depending
    on your preference and the condition of the eggplants
salt

Mushroom-Tomato Sauce

2 Tbs. olive oil
2 cups chopped onion
1 ¼ tsp. salt
1 ½ lbs. (or even 2 lbs.) mushrooms, coarsely chopped
5 medium cloves garlic, sliced or minced
1 14½-oz. can tomatoes, including all the liquid
1 6-oz. can tomato paste
1 tsp. cinnamon
lots of black pepper
1 tsp. each: oregano and basil
1 packed cup freshly minced parsley
½ cup fine bread crumbs, plus extra for the top
½ cup grated parmesan cheese

Béchamel Sauce

3 Tbs. butter
6 Tbs. flour
2 ½ cups hot milk (lowfat works fine!)
½ cup grated parmesan cheese, plus extra for the top
nutmeg

1) Slice the eggplants into quarter-inch-thick rounds. Salt the slices lightly on both sides, then layer them gently in a colander, and place over a sink or bowl. Let stand for 20 to 30 minutes. This will allow them to sweat out their bitter juices. (Meanwhile, you can work on the mushroom sauce.)

2) Lightly oil a baking sheet, and preheat oven to 375°F. Retrieve the eggplant slices from their spa, and pat them dry with a clean towel. Spread the slices on the tray (it's ok if they pile up a little) and bake until tender (20 to 25 minutes). Meanwhile, prepare the Béchamel sauce.

. . . . .

MUSHROOM-TOMATO SAUCE:

1) Heat the olive oil in a large, deep skillet or a Dutch oven. Add onions and salt, and cook over medium heat, stirring, for 8 to 10 minutes, or until the onions become translucent. Add mushrooms and garlic, stir, and cover. Cook over medium heat another 8 to 10 minutes.

2) Add tomatoes, tomato paste, cinnamon, pepper, oregano, and basil. (Use a spoon or a dinner knife to break the tomatoes into bite-sized pieces.) Bring to a boil, then lower heat, and simmer, uncovered, another 12 to 15 minutes. Remove from heat, and stir in parsley, bread crumbs, and parmesan. Set aside.

. . . . .

BÉCHAMEL SAUCE:

1) In a medium-sized saucepan, melt the butter over low heat. Whisk in 4 Tbs. of the flour, keeping up a steady motion with the whisk even after the flour is added. Cook for several minutes, whisking still.

2) Slowly pour in the hot milk, whisking even yet. Cook and stir over low heat another 5 to 8 minutes, or until the sauce is very smooth and thickened slightly. Sift in the remaining 2 Tbs. flour, whisking yet some more, to prevent lumps. After another 5 to 8 minutes of cooking with occasional stirring, add the parmesan and a few shakes of nutmeg. Remove from heat. The sauce should be smooth and quite thick.

. . . . .

ASSEMBLY: Preheat oven to 375°F. Oil a very large casserole or a deep oblong baking pan with dimensions of at least 9 x 13 inches. Place a double layer of eggplant on the bottom, and add the entire batch of mushroom sauce. Lay the remaining eggplant slices over the mushroom sauce, and spread the Béchamel over the top. Dust lightly with fine bread crumbs and a small handful or two of parmesan. Bake uncovered for 35 to 40 minutes, or until bubbly on the bottom and ever so lightly browned on top. Serve hot.

Lasagne

Preparation time:
1½ hours

Yield:
6 to 8 servings

Have ready:
1) 1 batch Italian Tomato Sauce ~ any variation (p. 80)
2) 12 lasagne noodles, half-cooked or even uncooked (it <u>will</u> work!)
3) 1½ to 2 cups ricotta or cottage cheese (lowfat OK)
4) 1 lb. grated or thinly sliced mozzarella cheese
5) at least ½ cup grated parmesan, romano, or asiago cheese
6) a 9 x 13-inch pan

Proceedings:
1) Preheat oven to 375°F.
2) Spread a little sauce over the bottom of the pan.
3) Cover with a single layer of noodles (⅓ of them. Break as necessary, to fit.)
4) Place mounds of ricotta/cottage cheese here and there. Use half.
5) Add ⅓ the sauce, followed by
6) ½ the mozzarella, randomly scattered, then
7) another ⅓ the noodles, and
8) the remaining ricotta (cottage), followed by
9) another ⅓ the sauce, which gets covered by
10) the remaining mozzarella.
11) Add every last noodle, and
12) the final sauce.
13) Sprinkle the parmesan (romano/asiago) over the top.

Bake for 45 minutes. Cover loosely with foil toward the end of the baking, if it is getting too brown. Let stand 10 minutes before serving.

1¼ hours to prepare (most of which is baking time). This assumes the tomato sauce is already made.

Eggplant Parmesan

Yield: at least 8 servings

Eggplant is highly absorbent, and when fried, it soaks up oil like a sponge. Because it is usually fried for Eggplant Parmesan, this dish ends up being much heavier than it needs to be. Here is a way to prepare crispy eggplant without frying ~ I suppose you could call it the shake-and-bake method. It is easier and much neater than frying, in addition to being lighter and better for you ~ and all those things you are possibly tired of hearing about. But people seem not to get tired of things tasting good, and this does taste really good.

2 medium globe eggplants (about 7 inches long)

¾ cup milk (more, as needed)

2 cups fine bread crumbs or wheat germ (or a combination)

1 tsp. basil

½ tsp. each: oregano and thyme

1 batch Italian Tomato Sauce (p.80)

1 lb. mozzarella cheese, thinly sliced or grated

parmesan cheese ~ about ½ cup (amount = flexible)

1) Preheat oven to 375°F. Lightly oil a baking tray and a 9 x 13-inch pan.

2) Cut the eggplants into ⊙'s ½ inch thick. Place the milk in a shallow bowl; combine bread crumbs (wheat germ) with herbs on a plate. Dip each eggplant slice in the milk, moistening both sides, then coat it thoroughly with the crumb mixture. Spread the prepared slices on the baking tray and the pan, and bake until tender (about 20 to 30 minutes). Remove from oven, and pile them gently on the baking tray.

3) Without cleaning the 9 x 13-inch pan, ladle some tomato sauce into the bottom. Add a layer of eggplant slices, and cover with more sauce. Arrange some mozzarella over the sauce, then repeat the layering until you run out of something or you run out of room, whichever comes first. Generously sprinkle the top with parmesan.

4) Bake uncovered at 375°F. for about 40 minutes, or until heated through and bubbly around the edges. Remove from oven and let sit about 10 minutes before serving. Serve hot or warm.

Tart & Tangy Baked Beans

Preparation time:
Presoaked beans need
up to 1½ hours to cook.
Get everything else
ready during
this time.

Yield:
6 to 8
Servings

A version of this recipe appeared in earlier editions as "Cheese-Beans". This one is more deeply seasoned, but basically the same. Cheese is optional.

Serve this with rice, corn bread (p. 114), or warmed tortillas (p. 115).

NOTE: The beans need to soak for at least 4 hours ahead of time.

3 cups dry pinto beans, soaked
4 cups chopped onions
2 Tbs. olive oil
1½ to 2 tsp. salt
1 Tbs. chili powder
2 tsp. cumin
1½ tsp. dry mustard
6 to 8 medium cloves garlic, minced
6 Tbs. dry white wine (optional)

6 to 8 Tbs. cider vinegar (to taste)
3 to 4 Tbs. molasses (to taste)
2 cups grated mild cheese (optional)
lots of black pepper
crushed red pepper, to taste
3 medium-sized tart apples, cut
   into medium-sized chunks
4 medium-sized ripe tomatoes,
   chopped

1) Place the presoaked beans in a kettle and cover them with plenty of water. Bring to a boil, lower to a simmer, partially cover, and cook slowly until tender (1¼ to 1½ hours), checking the water level during cooking. Drain off any excess when the beans are done. (This can be saved for soup stock.)

2) Begin cooking the onions in olive oil in a medium-sized skillet. Add salt, chili powder, cumin, and mustard, and sauté over medium heat for about 8 to 10 minutes. Add garlic, and sauté for another 5 minutes or so. Add this sauté to the cooked beans, along with all remaining ingredients.

3) Preheat oven to 350°F. Mix the beans well and transfer to a deep casserole or a 9 x 13-inch baking pan. Cover tightly with foil, and bake 1 hour.

Spinach-Rice Casserole

The original version contained 4 eggs. This one has only 2, and they're optional. Also, you can experiment by replacing some or all of the spinach with other greens: mustard, kale, collard, etc.

2 cups uncooked brown rice (long- or short-grain)
1 Tbs. butter or olive oil
2 cups minced onion
2 lbs. fresh spinach, stemmed and finely chopped
1 tsp. salt
4 to 5 medium cloves garlic, minced
1/4 tsp. nutmeg
1/4 tsp. cayenne
black pepper, to taste
optional: 1 to 2 tsp. prepared mustard
1/2 cup sunflower seeds
2 beaten eggs (optional)
1 cup lowfat milk (optional)
1 1/2 cups (packed) grated cheddar (optional)
paprika

1) Place the rice in a medium-sized saucepan with 3 cups water. Cover, bring to a boil, then lower to the slowest possible simmer. Cook, covered and undisturbed, for 35 to 40 minutes. Remove from heat, transfer to a medium-sized bowl, and fluff with a fork.

2) Preheat oven to 350°F. Oil a 9 X 13-inch baking pan.

3) Heat the butter or oil in a deep skillet. Add onion, and sauté 5 to 8 minutes ~ until soft. Add spinach, salt, and garlic, and cook about 5 minutes more over medium heat, stirring frequently. Add this to the rice, along with the seasonings and half the sunflower seeds. Mix well.

4) PURELY OPTIONAL: Beat together eggs and milk, and stir this into the spinach-rice mixture, along with the grated cheese.

5) Spread into the prepared pan, sprinkle with the remaining sunflower seeds and dust with paprika. Bake uncovered for 35 to 40 minutes ~until heated through and lightly browned on top.

Solyanka

1¼ hours to prepare
(including baking)

Serves about 6

Very simple ingredients comprise this tasty casserole. Serve it with Beet Borscht (p. 35) or Odessa Beets (p. 68) and Balkan Cucumber Salad (p. 69).

4 medium potatoes (about 2 lbs.)
1½ cups cottage cheese (lowfat ok)
1 cup firm yogurt
1 Tbs. butter
2 cups chopped onion
¾ to 1 tsp. salt
1 tsp. caraway seeds
1 small head green cabbage, shredded (about 6 cups)

2 medium carrots, shredded
4 to 5 medium cloves garlic, minced
1 Tbs. dill (3 Tbs., if using fresh)
lots of black pepper, to taste
3 Tbs. cider vinegar
½ cup sunflower seeds } toppings
paprika

1) Preheat oven to 350°F. Lightly grease a 2-quart casserole or its equivalent.
2) Scrub the potatoes, cut them into small pieces, and boil until mashable. (You can do Steps 4 and 5 while the potatoes boil.) Drain and transfer to a large bowl.
3) Mash the potatoes while still hot, adding cottage cheese and yogurt.
4) Melt the butter in a large, deep skillet. Add onions and salt, and sauté about 5 minutes. Add caraway and cabbage, and sauté about 10 more minutes, stirring occasionally and covering in between.
5) When the cabbage is tender, add carrots, garlic, and dill. Cook about 5 more minutes, and remove from heat.
6) Add the sautéed vegetables and all remaining ingredients -except toppings- to the mashed potatoes. Mix well and spread into the prepared pan. Sprinkle the sunflower seeds and paprika on top.
7) Bake uncovered 35 to 45 minutes, or until heated through and lightly browned on top. Serve hot.

MEXICAN PEPPER CASSEROLE

If you want to serve this with beans and rice, don't forget to get them ready beforehand.

1 Tbs. olive oil

2 cups sliced onion

6 to 8 medium-sized bell peppers (a mix of colors, if available), thinly sliced

4 to 5 medium cloves garlic, minced

1 tsp. salt

1½ tsp. cumin

optional: 1 tsp. dried coriander

1 tsp. dry mustard

black pepper, to taste

cayenne, to taste

2 Tbs. flour

2 to 3 eggs

2 cups yogurt and/or sour cream

optional: a handful of freshly minced cilantro

2 cups sliced jack or cheddar cheese (optional)

paprika, for the top

1) Lightly grease a 10-inch square pan or its equivalent. Preheat oven to 375°F.

2) Heat the olive oil in a deep skillet or Dutch oven. Add onions and sauté about 5 to 8 minutes over medium heat, until the onions begin to soften.

3) Add peppers, salt, cumin, dried coriander, mustard, black pepper, and cayenne. Sauté another 8 to 10 minutes, then sprinkle in the flour. Cook and stir another 5 minutes, or until the peppers are very tender. Transfer to the baking pan.

4) Beat together the eggs and yogurt or sour cream. Stir in the minced fresh cilantro. Pour this custard over the peppers. Top with slices of cheese, if desired, and dust with paprika.

5) Bake uncovered for 40 to 45 minutes until firm in the center and bubbly around the edges. Serve hot with rice and beans and/or warmed tortillas.

BULGARIAN PEPPER CASSEROLE

❋ ❋ ❋

Yield: enough
to feed at least
6 to 8

Garlicky herbed sautéed peppers and onions are blended with feta cheese, dilled lemon rice, and whipped cottage or ricotta cheese, then topped with tomatoes, olives, and more garlic, and baked until bubbly hot.

The peppers can be sautéed and the rice prepared several days in advance. Assemble and bake the casserole just before serving.

❋ ❋ ❋ ❋ ❋ ❋ ❋ ❋ ❋ ❋ ❋ ❋ ❋ ❋ ❋ ❋

1½ cups uncooked brown rice
2¾ cups water
1 Tbs. lemon juice
2 to 3 Tbs. freshly minced dill (or 2 tsp. dried dill)
2 Tbs. olive oil
2 cups minced onion
4 to 5 medium green and/or red bell peppers, chopped into ½-inch pieces
¾ tsp. salt (more, to taste)
fresh black pepper
½ tsp. oregano
2 tsp. basil
8 medium cloves garlic, half of them minced, half of them sliced
    (keep minced and sliced garlic separate)
1 cup crumbled feta cheese
1½ cups cottage or ricotta cheese (may be lowfat)
2 medium-sized fresh, ripe tomatoes
1 cup whole Niçoise olives (or sliced, pitted Kalamata olives)
    (possibly more, to taste)

1) Place rice and water in a saucepan. Cover and bring to a boil. Turn the heat down as low as possible, and simmer without interruption for about 40 minutes, or until the rice is tender. Remove from heat, fluff with a fork, and stir in lemon juice and dill. Set aside.

2) Meanwhile, heat the olive oil in a large skillet. Add onions, and sauté over medium heat 5 to 8 minutes, or until the onions become soft. Add peppers, salt, pepper, and herbs, and continue to cook, stirring occasionally, for about 10 more minutes, or until the peppers are tender. Stir in the minced garlic (save the sliced garlic for later) and cook for just a minute more. Remove from heat, and stir in the feta cheese.

3) When you are ready to assemble the casserole, preheat the oven to 375°F. Lightly oil a 9 x 13-inch baking pan.

4) Place the cottage or ricotta cheese in a blender or food processor fitted with the steel blade, and whip until smooth.

5) Combine rice, pepper sauté, and whipped cheese in a large bowl, and mix until very well combined. Transfer to the prepared pan, and spread into place. Top with tomato slices, then scatter olives and slices of garlic in a liberated, random fashion over the tomatoes.

6) Bake uncovered at 375°F. until bubbly ~ about 30 to 40 minutes. Serve hot or warm.

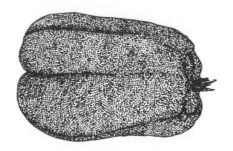

Arabian Squash Casserole

Preparation time: about
1 hour, after the squash
is cooked and puréed

Good served with Tabouli
Salad (p.46), or with warmed
pita bread and a spinach
salad with ripe tomatoes.

Yield
4 to 5 servings

4 cups cooked squash or pumpkin, mashed or puréed
2 Tbs. olive oil
1½ cups chopped onion
1 tsp. salt
2 small bell peppers (one red and one green, if possible), minced
4 or 5 medium cloves garlic, minced
black pepper and cayenne, to taste
½ cup firm yogurt
1 cup crumbled feta cheese
OPTIONAL: sunflower seeds and/or minced walnuts, for the top

PRELIMINARY: Preheat oven to 375°F.

1) Place the mashed or puréed squash in a large bowl.

2) Heat the olive oil in a medium-sized skillet. Add onion, and sauté
   over medium heat for about 5 minutes. Add salt and bell peppers.
   Sauté about 5 more minutes, or until the peppers begin to get soft.

3) Add garlic, black pepper, and cayenne, and sauté a few more minutes.

4) Add the sauté, along with yogurt and feta, to the squash, and mix well.
   Spread into an ungreased 9-inch square baking pan; sprinkle the top
   lightly with sunflower seeds and/or minced walnuts.

5) Bake uncovered for 25 to 30 minutes, or until bubbly.

Chilean Squash (a variation)

Delete: yogurt, feta, sunflower seeds, walnuts.

Add to step 2: 1 tsp. cumin, ½ tsp. dried coriander (optional), 1 tsp.
chili powder, 2 cups corn (frozen/defrosted = OK)

Top with: 1 cup grated cheddar

Preparation time:
1¼ hours after
soybeans are soaked

SCHEHERAZADE CASSEROLE

This is one of my favorite recipes, and I strongly recommend it: ground soybeans baked with bulgur, vegetables, garlic, tomatoes, feta cheese. The texture is deeply satisfying, and the seasonings are bold. It tastes great!

Few changes have been made from the original, other than to intensify the seasonings. It was — and remains — eggless.

You can assemble the casserole a day or 2 in advance of baking it. Also, it can be frozen before or after baking. It doesn't mind being reheated.

PRELIMINARY: The soybeans need at least 4 hours to soak beforehand.

1 cup raw bulgur
1 cup boiling water
2 Tbs. olive oil
2 cups minced onion
3 large cloves garlic, minced
½ tsp. salt
2 tsp. cumin
1½ tsp. basil

black pepper and cayenne, to taste
1 large bell pepper, diced
¾ cup dry soybeans, soaked
1 14½-oz. can tomatoes, drained
3 Tbs. (half a small can) tomato paste
½ cup (packed) finely minced parsley
1½ to 2 cups crumbled feta cheese

1) Preheat oven to 375°F. Lightly oil a 9 x 13-inch baking pan.

2) Place the bulgur in a small bowl. Add boiling water, cover with a plate, and let stand at least 15 minutes.

3) Meanwhile, heat the olive oil in a large skillet. Add onion, garlic, salt, and seasonings. Stir occasionally as you sauté over medium heat for 5 to 8 minutes. Add bell pepper and sauté about 5 minutes more.

4) Drain the soybeans, if necessary, and place them in a blender or food processor with 1 cup fresh water. Grind until the soybeans resemble a coarse batter. Transfer to a large bowl.

5) Add the soaked bulgur and sautéed vegetables to the soybeans. Stir in the tomatoes, breaking them up into bite-sized pieces. Add tomato paste, parsley, and 1 cup of the feta. Mix well.

6) Spread into the baking pan and sprinkle the remaining feta on top. Cover and bake for 30 minutes at 375°F, then uncover and bake 15 minutes more with the oven turned down to 350°F. Serve hot.

Preparation time:
The batter takes a few minutes. Cooking the crêpes takes about 15 minutes.

Yield: 8 to 10 (7-inch crêpes)

Elegant, but not extravagant, these thin pancakes are at the same time sturdy and delicate. You can make them just to have around. Keep them stacked on a plate, tightly covered and refrigerated. They will last at least a week — just fill and heat as desired. Wrap crêpes around many varieties of foods (a great way to use leftovers!) for different occasions, different times of day. They can quickly transform otherwise ordinary food into something special.

> 1 large egg
> 1¼ cups milk (can be lowfat)
> 1 cup flour
> ¼ tsp. salt
> a few drops of oil for the pan

NOTE: You will need a 6- or 7-inch crêpe or omelette pan — ideally a heavy one with a nonstick surface.

1) Place egg, milk, flour, and salt in a blender or food processor, and whip until smooth.

2) Heat a crêpe or omelette pan. After a few minutes, lightly brush its entire inside surface with oil. When the pan is hot enough to sizzle a drop of water instantly on contact, pour in approximately ¼ cup batter. Slowly tilt the pan in all directions until the batter thoroughly coats the bottom. Pour off any excess batter (the pancake should be thin). Cook on one side over medium heat until set (about 20 seconds), then turn over and cook for just another second or two on the other side.

3) Turn the crêpe out onto a clean, dry dinner plate, and repeat the pro-cedure until you have used up all the batter. (If you keep the pan hot, you won't have to add any additional oil.) You can pile the finished crêpes on the plate — they won't stick together.

4) Cover the plate tightly with plastic wrap, and refrigerate until use. The crêpes will keep well for at least several days.

5) To fill, simply place a small amount of whatever filling at one end of the crêpe and fold over sides and end to make a neat little packet. Filled crêpes can be heated gently — covered, in a 325°F oven — or sautéed in a little butter just before serving.

SUGGESTED FILLINGS

FOR DESSERT:
- Sauté in butter, fold in quarters, and sprinkle with powdered sugar.
- Lightly sauté some slices of tart apple; drizzle with lemon juice, cinnamon, and a little maple syrup or honey. Fill the crêpes and serve warm — plain, or with ice cream or whipped cream.
- Heat crêpes gently and serve with room-temperature Berry Sauce (p.207) — with or without ice cream.

VEGETABLES:
- Steamed whole green beans with almonds
- Steamed asparagus or broccoli spears with Zippy Cheese Sauce (p. 92), Rarebit (p. 93), or a Vegetable Purée (p.86)
- Steamed carrot sticks with Cashew-Ginger Sauce (p. 90)

LEFTOVERS:
- White Rabbit Salad (p.48) — inside room-temperature crêpes
- Ratatouille (p.179) or Vegetable Stew (p.177)
- Stellar Mushroom Sauce (p.78)
- Asparagus-Mushroom Sauce (p.77) — delete water
- Caramelized Onion Sauce (p.78)
- Etc. (whatever ideas you come up with are probably just brilliant)

Zucchini-Feta Pancakes

...Light and very satisfying (also quite attractive, with lovely flecks of green). A food processor will grate the zucchini in seconds flat.

4 eggs, separated
4 packed cups coarsely grated zucchini (about four 7-inchers)
1 cup finely crumbled feta cheese
½ cup finely minced scallions
1 tsp. dried mint (or 1 Tbs. fresh, finely minced)
a little salt (optional, to taste)
lots of black pepper
⅓ cup flour
oil for frying
sour cream or yogurt for topping

1) Beat the egg whites until stiff.

2) In a medium-sized bowl, combine zucchini, egg yolks (or not), feta, scallions, seasonings, and flour. Mix well.

3) Fold the egg whites into the zucchini mixture.

4) Heat a little oil in a heavy skillet. When it is very hot, add spoonfuls of batter, and fry on both sides until golden and crisp.

5) Serve immediately, topped with sour cream or yogurt.

Cottage Cheese & Apple Pancakes

Preparation time:
30 minutes

Yield: serves
about 4

Great for brunch!

The batter keeps well for days, so you can have it on hand for breakfast cheer on an otherwise depressing weekday. (And these pancakes are equally uplifting for dinner.)

4 eggs, separated (yolks optional — use all, some, or none)
1 cup cottage cheese (lowfat OK)
1 cup (packed) grated tart apple
3/4 cup flour
1 to 2 tsp. lemon juice
optional: 1 Tbs. honey
1/2 tsp. cinnamon
1/2 tsp. salt
optional: 2 to 3 Tbs. finely minced walnuts or almonds
oil or butter for frying
real maple syrup   ⎫
sour cream or yogurt   ⎬ optional toppings
Berry Sauce (p. 207)   ⎭

1) Beat the egg whites until stiff.

2) Combine all other ingredients (except toppings and frying oil) in a medium-sized bowl and mix well. Fold in the egg whites.

3) Heat oil or melt butter in a skillet. When it is hot enough to sizzle a drop of batter on contact, add spoonfuls of batter. Fry on both sides until firm and lightly browned. Serve right away, topped with syrup, sour cream or yogurt, and /or Berry Sauce.

SWEET POTATO PANCAKES

30 minutes to prepare   Yield: 4 to 6 servings

   These can be for breakfast, brunch, lunch, or supper, depending on what you serve them with (and, of course, what time of day or night it is).

   The sweet potatoes and onion can be grated by hand or in a food processor fitted with the grating attachment. Peeling the sweet potatoes is optional. If you choose not to peel, scrub.

   NOTE: The batter stores well for several days if kept in a tightly covered container in the refrigerator.

4 cups (packed) coarsely grated sweet potatoes
        (approximately 1 large or 2 medium)
½ cup grated onion
3 to 4 Tbs lemon juice
1 tsp. salt
black pepper, to taste
4 beaten eggs
⅓ cup flour
optional: ¼ cup minced parsley
oil for frying
TOPPINGS: sour cream or yogurt
            applesauce

1) Combine all ingredients and mix well.

2) Heat a small amount of oil in a skillet until it is very hot. (It should sizzle a fleck of batter upon contact.)

3) Use a non-slotted spoon to form thin pancakes, patting the batter down. Fry on both sides until brown, adding small amounts of additional oil, if/as needed.

4) Serve hot, with toppings.

35 minutes to prepare;
1 hour to chill;
15 minutes to cook

Lentil-Walnut Burgers

These are delicious fried or broiled, with or without some cheese melted on top. Try serving Lentil-Walnut Burgers with thickly sliced, very ripe homegrown tomatoes and Faux Aioli (p. 91).

NOTES: ☆ You can sauté the vegetables while the lentils cook. ☆ The burgers can be made up to several days in advance and stored in the refrigerator until just before cooking. ☆ Uncooked burgers can be individually wrapped and frozen. Defrost before cooking.

¾ cup dry lentils
1½ cups water
2 Tbs. cider vinegar
1 Tbs. peanut or olive oil
1 cup finely minced onion
4 to 5 large cloves garlic, minced
about 10 large mushrooms, minced
½ cup very finely minced walnuts
1 tsp. salt
OPTIONAL: ½ lb. fresh spinach, finely minced
1 tsp. dry mustard
fresh black pepper, to taste
½ cup fine bread crumbs or wheat germ

1) Place lentils and water in a small saucepan and bring to a boil. Lower the heat and simmer, partially covered, for about 30 minutes, or until the lentils are soft and the liquid is gone. Transfer to a medium-sized bowl, add vinegar, and mash well.

2) Heat oil in a medium-sized skillet. Add onions and sauté over medium heat for about 5 minutes. Add all remaining ingredients except wheat germ or bread crumbs, and sauté 5 to 10 minutes, or until all the vegetables are tender. Add the sauté and crumbs to the lentils and mix well. Chill for about 1 hour before forming patties.

3) Form 4-inch-diameter burgers. Fry in a small amount of hot oil on both sides until heated through and crispy on the outside, or broil for 5 to 8 minutes on each side.

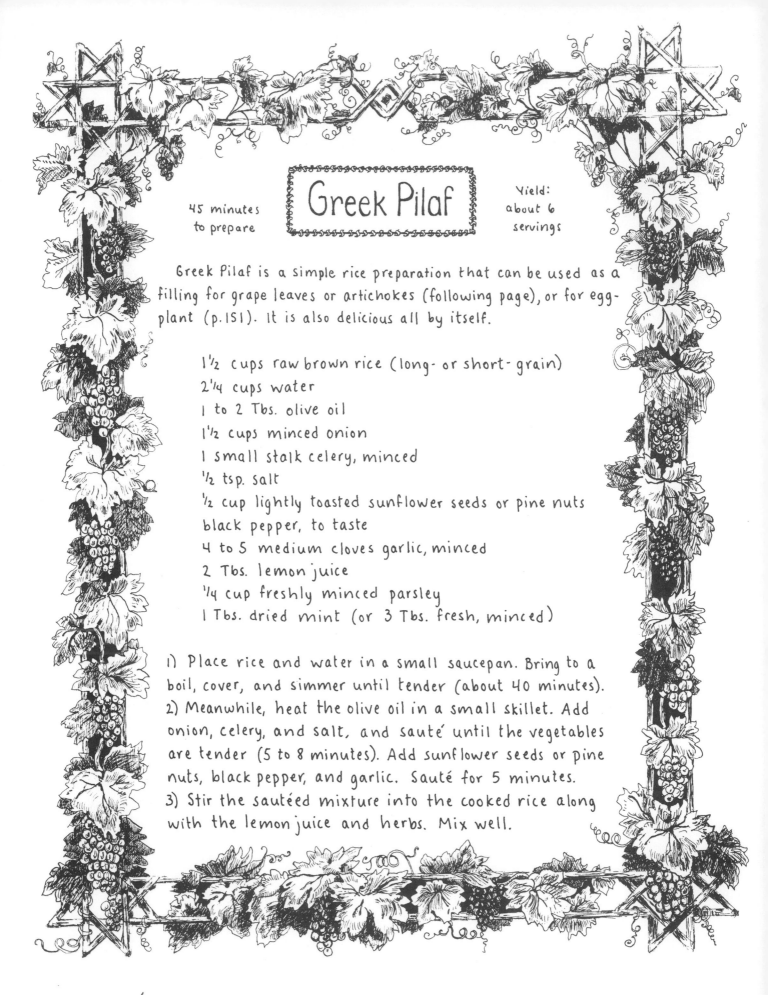

Greek Pilaf

45 minutes to prepare

Yield: about 6 servings

Greek Pilaf is a simple rice preparation that can be used as a filling for grape leaves or artichokes (following page), or for eggplant (p.151). It is also delicious all by itself.

1½ cups raw brown rice (long- or short- grain)
2¼ cups water
1 to 2 Tbs. olive oil
1½ cups minced onion
1 small stalk celery, minced
½ tsp. salt
½ cup lightly toasted sunflower seeds or pine nuts
black pepper, to taste
4 to 5 medium cloves garlic, minced
2 Tbs. lemon juice
¼ cup freshly minced parsley
1 Tbs. dried mint (or 3 Tbs. fresh, minced)

1) Place rice and water in a small saucepan. Bring to a boil, cover, and simmer until tender (about 40 minutes).
2) Meanwhile, heat the olive oil in a small skillet. Add onion, celery, and salt, and sauté until the vegetables are tender (5 to 8 minutes). Add sunflower seeds or pine nuts, black pepper, and garlic. Sauté for 5 minutes.
3) Stir the sautéed mixture into the cooked rice along with the lemon juice and herbs. Mix well.

Stuffed Grape Leaves

These can be served with an assortment of other dishes to make an appetizer sampler that is really main-course material (see Mezza, p. 100). You can also serve Stuffed Grape Leaves as a light entrée with any soup, especially Lentil Soup (p. 25).

If you have grapevines in your yard, pick leaves for stuffing early in the season, when they are large enough to stuff, but still tender. You can also buy preserved leaves in specialty shops or in the imported foods section of a good grocery store.

1 recipe Greek Pilaf (preceding page)
about 24 grape leaves (3 to 4 inches across)
1 batch Greek Lemon Sauce (p. 91)

1) Preheat oven to 325°F. Lightly oil a baking tray.
2) Place each leaf down flat on a clean surface. Add a heaping tablespoon of filling near the stem end. Roll tightly, folding in the sides.
3) Arrange the stuffed leaves on the prepared tray. Bake about 20 minutes or until heated through. You can also skip this step and just serve them cold, with the sauce on top or on the side. Serves 4 to 6.

to Stuff an Artichoke

1 recipe Greek Pilaf (preceding page)
6 medium artichokes
1 batch Greek Lemon Sauce (p. 91) or
    Horseradish Sauce (also on p. 91)

1) Trim and cook the artichokes as you normally would. Drain and cool until handleable.
2) Pull off the centermost leaf cluster. Use a teaspoon to scoop out the fibrous choke, being careful not to scoop out the tender heart beneath it. Fill the cavity with pilaf. Serve at room temperature, with sauce for dipping. Serves 6.

STUFFED EGGPLANT

45 minutes to prepare;
30 to 40 minutes to bake

Yield: 6 servings
per recipe

I. 1970s ALTERNATIVE LIFESTYLE-STYLE — still good!

3 medium globe eggplants
(about 7 inches long)

2 Tbs. olive oil

2 cups minced onion

½ lb. mushrooms, chopped

1 tsp. salt (or more, to taste)

2 tsp. basil

a dash of thyme

1 tsp. oregano

fresh black pepper, to taste

5 to 6 medium cloves garlic, minced

2 cups cooked brown rice

1½ cups cottage cheese (lowfat ok)

1 cup grated cheddar

½ cup (packed) freshly minced parsley

Tabasco and soy sauce, to taste

a handful of sunflower seeds

a handful of sesame seeds

paprika

Red Pepper Purée (p.86) -optional

1) Cut the eggplants in half lengthwise. Use a spoon to scoop out the insides, leaving a ½-inch shell. Mince the eggplant scoopings.
2) Heat the olive oil in a large skillet. Add onion, mushrooms, salt, herbs, and pepper. Sauté over medium heat for about 5 minutes, then add the minced eggplant. Cook until the eggplant is tender (about 15 minutes), stirring occasionally. Add garlic, and sauté for about 5 more minutes. Transfer to a large bowl.
3) Add rice, cheeses, parsley, Tabasco, and soy sauce, and mix well. Taste to correct seasonings.
4) Preheat oven to 375°F. Fill the eggplant shells, and top with seeds and a fine dusting of paprika. Bake for 30 to 40 minutes — until heated through. Serve hot, with room-temperature Red Pepper Purée drizzled on top, for a lovely effect.

II. MEDITERRANEAN STYLE

3 medium eggplants (about 7 inches long)

a double recipe Greek Pilaf (p. 148)

1 cup crumbled feta cheese

3 medium-sized ripe tomatoes

1) Preheat oven to 375°F. Slice eggplants in half lengthwise, and bake face-down until tender (20 to 30 minutes). Scoop out and mince the insides.
2) Combine chopped eggplant with Greek Pilaf. Stir in the feta. Stuff the eggplant shells and top with slices of tomato.
3) Turn oven down to 350°, and bake until heated through (about 30 minutes).

Stuffed Squash

Each of these filling recipes makes plenty for 4 servings of Stuffed Squash — half a medium-sized squash apiece. Any winter squash will work; the most common are acorn and butternut.

The 2 squash need to be prebaked. Preheat the oven to 350°F. Split the squash lengthwise down the middle and remove the seeds. Bake face-down on an oiled tray for about 30 minutes or until very soft (a fork should slide in easily). Make your choice of fillings while the squash bake.

I. SAVORY FRUIT-STUFFED SQUASH

2 medium-sized winter squash, halved lengthwise and prebaked
1 cup raw brown rice (long- or short-grain) + 1¾ cups water

1 Tbs. butter
1½ cups minced onion
2 medium cloves garlic, minced
2 medium-sized tart apples, diced
3 large navel oranges, sectioned
½ tsp. cinnamon
½ tsp. allspice or cloves

1 tsp. salt
1 to 2 Tbs. honey or brown sugar
1 cup chopped almonds and/or pecans
TOPPINGS:
Orange-Ginger Sauce (p. 90)
yogurt

1) Place rice and water in a small saucepan. Bring to a boil, cover, and let simmer undisturbed for 30 to 40 minutes — until tender. Transfer to a medium-sized bowl.

2) Meanwhile, melt butter in a medium skillet. Add onion and sauté for about 5 minutes, or until translucent.

3) Add garlic, apples, oranges, and spices, and sauté over medium heat about 5 minutes more. The orange sections may fall apart, but that's OK.

4) Add the sauté to the rice and mix well. Season to taste with salt and honey or brown sugar.

5) Preheat oven to 350°F. Fill the prebaked squash halves, and top with chopped nuts. Bake uncovered until heated through — about 20 to 30 minutes (depending on how warm the ingredients were to begin with).

. . . .
. . . .

II. COMPREHENSIVELY STUFFED SQUASH

Perfect for a holiday meal, especially Thanksgiving. For a colorful accompaniment, choose Odessa Beets (p.68) or Vegetable Purées (Beet or Red Pepper – p.86) to go alongside or on top.

2 medium-sized winter squash, halved and prebaked
2 Tbs. butter
1 cup minced onion
½ lb. mushrooms, minced
1 large clove garlic, minced
1 stalk celery, minced
½ tsp. salt
lots of black pepper
½ tsp. sage
½ tsp. thyme
2 Tbs. lemon juice
¼ cup minced walnuts
¼ cup sunflower seeds
¼ cup raisins (optional)
2 cups good bread crumbs (from good bread)
6 to 8 dried apricots
1 cup (packed) grated cheddar (entirely optional)

1) Melt the butter in a large skillet. Add onion, and sauté over medium heat for about 5 minutes, or until the onion is translucent.

2) Add mushrooms, garlic, celery, and seasonings, and sauté about 10 minutes — until everything is tender and well mingled.

3) Stir in remaining ingredients and mix well. Taste to correct seasonings.

4) Preheat oven to 350°F. Fill the prebaked squash and bake, covered, until heated through (20 to 30 minutes).

⌣Zuccanoes⌣
(Stuffed Zucchini)

PRELIMINARY: You'll need 1½ cups cooked rice.

4 medium-sized zucchini (about 2 lbs.)
1 to 2 Tbs. olive oil
1½ cups minced onion
1 tsp. salt
½ lb. mushrooms, minced
6 medium cloves garlic, minced
1½ cups cooked rice (any kind)
1½ cups minced almonds or pecans, lightly toasted
3 Tbs. fresh lemon juice
black pepper and cayenne, to taste
a few pinches of freshly minced — or dried — herbs:
 ~ any combination of parsley, basil, dill, thyme, or marjoram
1 cup (packed) grated Swiss or cheddar cheese
1 batch Vegetable Purée (pages 86 & 87) — OPTIONAL

1) Cut the zucchini lengthwise down the middle. Use a smallish spoon to scoop out the insides, leaving a canoe with a ¼-inch shell. Mince the insides, and set everything aside.

2) Heat the olive oil in a medium-sized skillet. Add the onion and salt, and sauté over medium heat until the onion is soft (5 to 8 minutes).

3) Add the minced zucchini innards and the mushrooms. Turn up the heat and cook for about 8 minutes, stirring, letting the liquid evaporate. Stir in the garlic and remove from heat.

4) Stir in the rice and nuts, along with the lemon juice, and season to taste with black pepper, cayenne, and the herbs of your choice.

5) Preheat oven to 350°F. Fill the zucchini shells, top with cheese, and bake for 30 to 40 minutes, or until heated through. Serve hot, sauced with a lovely Vegetable Purée, if desired.

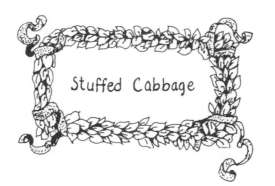

Stuffed Cabbage

Preparation time:
  1½ hours
(This includes time
for making the sauce.)

Yield:
6 servings
(2 rolls apiece)

Serve over rice.

1 large head green cabbage
1 Tbs. butter
1 cup minced onion
1 small clove garlic, minced
1 stalk celery, minced
1 small carrot, diced
¾ cup minced cashews (optional)
¼ cup sunflower seeds

salt and black pepper, to taste
2 cups (1 lb.) ricotta cheese
1 small tart apple, finely chopped
¼ cup raisins or currants
3 to 4 Tbs. lemon juice
1 to 2 Tbs. soy sauce
1 Tbs. honey (optional)
1 batch Cashew-Ginger Sauce (p.90)

1) Heat a large kettleful of water to boiling. Core the head of cabbage, and carefully lower it into the water. Turn the heat down to a simmer, and leave the cabbage in there for about 10 to 15 minutes, or until the outer leaves can be removed easily. Retrieve the cabbage from the water, and pull off the 12 outermost leaves. Make sure the cabbage is cooked well enough so the leaves will not break when rolled, but not so well done that they disintegrate. Set aside the 12 leaves, and save the rest of the cabbage to use for another dish. (It's great for soup!)

2) Melt the butter in a medium-sized skillet and add the onion, garlic, celery, and carrot. Sauté over medium heat for about 10 minutes, then add nuts, seeds, salt, and pepper. When the vegetables are tender, remove from heat.

3) Place the ricotta in a medium-large bowl. Add the sauté, plus the apple, raisins, lemon juice, soy sauce, and optional honey. Mix well, and taste to adjust seasonings. Meanwhile, preheat oven to 325°F.

4) Place 3 to 4 Tbs. filling near the base of each cabbage leaf. Roll firmly, folding in the sides. Arrange the cabbage rolls in an oblong baking pan, pour Cashew-Ginger Sauce over the top and bake, covered, until heated through — about 30 minutes.

Spinach-Ricotta Pie

40 minutes to prepare;
40 to 45 more to bake

Yield:
4 to 6 servings

The Crust: 6 Tbs. butter, cut into small pieces
1 ½ cups flour
about 4 Tbs. cold water, milk, or buttermilk

The Filling: 1 tsp. butter
1 cup minced onion
1 lb. spinach, stemmed and finely chopped
½ tsp. salt
freshly ground pepper, to taste
1 tsp. basil
1 lb. ricotta cheese
2 or 3 beaten eggs
3 Tbs. flour
½ cup (packed) grated sharp cheese of your choice
a dash of nutmeg (optional)
Optional topping: 1 cup sour cream (may be lowfat), lightly beaten
paprika

CRUST

1) Use a pastry cutter, two forks, or a food processor to cut together the butter and flour until the mixture is uniformly blended and resembles coarse cornmeal. (The food processor will do this in just a few spurts.)

2) Add just enough liquid (water, milk, or buttermilk) to hold the dough together. Roll out the dough and form a crust in a 9- or 10-inch pie pan. Set aside.

3) Preheat oven to 375°F. Melt the butter in a medium-sized skillet, add the onion, and sauté for 5 minutes over medium heat. Add spinach, salt, pepper, and basil, and cook, stirring, over medium-high heat until the spinach is wilted. Remove from heat.

4) Combine all filling ingredients in a large bowl, and mix well. Spread into the unbaked pie shell. For an extra rich pie, top with sour cream, spread to the edges of the crust. Dust generously with paprika.

5) Bake 40 to 45 minutes, or until firm to the touch at the center. Serve hot, warm, or at room temperature.

Swiss Cheese & Mushroom Quiche

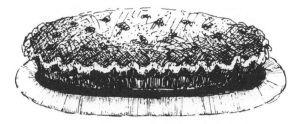

Preparation time: about 1¼ hours, including baking

Yield: one 10-inch pie (4 to 6 servings)

1 (10-inch) pie crust (recipe on preceding page), pressed into either a pie pan or a springform tart pan

1 tsp. butter

1½ cups chopped onion

¼ lb. mushrooms, sliced or minced

½ tsp. salt

black pepper

a pinch of thyme

½ tsp. dry mustard

4 large eggs (or 2 whole eggs plus 2 egg whites)

1½ cups milk (can be lowfat)

2 Tbs. flour

1½ cups (packed) grated Swiss cheese

paprika

OPTIONAL VARIATIONS:
* substitute other delicious cheeses for the Swiss
* add fresh tomato slices (no need to sauté first)
* minced fresh herbs (chives, parsley, chervil, marjoram, basil, dill, etc.)
* a hint of Hot: 1 tsp. prepared horseradish and/or cayenne or Tabasco

1) Preheat oven to 375°F.

2) Melt the butter in a small pan. Add onions, and sauté over medium heat for a few minutes. When they begin to soften, add mushrooms, salt, pepper, thyme, and mustard. Sauté about 5 minutes more and remove from heat.

3) Combine eggs, milk, and flour in a blender or food processor, and beat well.

4) Spread the grated cheese over the bottom of the unbaked crust, and spread the onion-mushroom mixture on top. Pour in the custard, and sprinkle the top with paprika.

5) Bake for 35 to 45 minutes, or until solid in the center. Serve hot, warm, or at room temperature.

Old Country Pie

1 unbaked 9- or 10-inch pie crust (see 2 pages back)
1 Tbs. butter or oil
1½ cups minced onion
1 tsp. caraway seeds
1 tsp. salt
½ lb. mushrooms, chopped or sliced
1½ cups shredded cabbage
1 medium stalk broccoli, chopped
1 medium carrot, thinly sliced
2 tsp. dill
lots of black pepper
3 medium cloves garlic, minced
2 Tbs. flour
½ cup cottage cheese (lowfat OK)
2 eggs (one or both yolks can be omitted)
2 medium scallions, finely minced
OPTIONAL: ¾ cup sour cream and/or yogurt; paprika

1) Prepare pie crust. Preheat oven to 350°F.
2) Melt butter (or heat oil) in a medium-sized skillet. Add onion, caraway, and salt, and sauté over medium heat until the onions begin to brown (10 to 15 minutes).
3) Add mushrooms, cabbage, broccoli, carrot, and dill, and sauté until everything is just tender — about 8 more minutes.
4) Stir in black pepper, garlic, and flour, and cook, stirring, for just a few minutes more. Remove from heat.
5) Beat together cottage cheese and eggs. Add this to the sauté along with the scallions and mix well.
6) Spread into the unbaked crust and, if desired, top with a layer of sour cream and/or yogurt. Sprinkle with paprika, and bake for 40 minutes or until set. Serve hot, warm, or at room temperature.

Cauliflower-Cheese Pie
with Grated Potato Crust

1 hour
to prepare

one 9-inch pie
(4 to 5 servings)

CONVENIENCE TIPS: ☆ Use food processor with grating attachment to grate cheese, potato, and onion in that order. (No need to clean in between.)
☆ Prepare the filling while the crust bakes.

CRUST:

2 cups (packed) grated raw potato
¼ cup grated onion
½ tsp. salt

1 egg white, lightly beaten
flour for your fingers
a little oil

FILLING:

1 Tbs. olive oil or butter
1 cup chopped onion
2 medium cloves garlic, minced
½ tsp. salt
black pepper, to taste
½ tsp. basil

¼ tsp. thyme
1 medium cauliflower, in small pieces
2 eggs
¼ cup milk (lowfat OK)
1 cup (packed) grated cheddar
paprika

1) Preheat oven to 400°F. Oil a 9-inch pie pan.

2) Combine grated potato and onion, salt, and egg white in a small bowl and mix well. Transfer to the pie pan and pat into place with lightly floured fingers, building up the sides into a handsome edge.

3) Bake for 30 minutes, then brush the crust with a little oil and bake it 10 more minutes. Remove from oven, and turn the temperature down to 375°F.

4) Heat the olive oil or butter in a large skillet. Add onion, garlic, salt, pepper, and herbs, and sauté over medium heat for about 5 minutes. Add cauliflower, stir, and cover. Cook until tender, stirring occasionally (about 8 to 10 minutes).

5) Spread half the cheese onto the baked crust (OK if it's still hot). Spoon the sautéed vegetables on top, then sprinkle on the remaining cheese. Beat the eggs and milk together, and pour this over the top. Dust lightly with paprika.

6) Bake 35 to 40 minutes, or until set. Serve hot or warm.

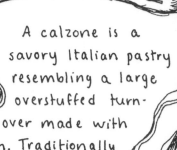

CALZONE

A calzone is a savory Italian pastry resembling a large overstuffed turn-over made with pizza dough. Traditionally, the filling is a mixture of cheeses, contrasting perfectly with the crispy crust.

I've included a cheese filling, plus a few ideas for nondairy ones as well.

One calzone per person plus a green salad make a very satisfying dinner.

Preparation time:
about 2 hours

Yield:
6 servings

- Make the filling while the dough rises, to save time.
- The dough can be made in advance and refrigerated or even frozen until use. Let come to room temperature before assembling, then knead for a few minutes to warm it up.

THE DOUGH:

1 cup wrist-temperature water
1½ tsp. active dry yeast
1 Tbs. honey or sugar
1½ tsp. salt
2½ to 3 cups flour
olive oil

1) Place the water in a medium-sized bowl. Sprinkle in the yeast, and stir in the honey or sugar until everything dissolves.

2) Use a whisk to stir in the salt and flour. When it gets too thick to whisk, mix with one floured hand. Knead in the bowl for about 5 minutes.

3) Brush a little olive oil over the dough, cover the bowl, and let rise in a warm place until doubled in bulk (about 1 hour). In the mean-time, you can get the filling ready.

SPINACH-CHEESE FILLING:

1 Tbs. olive oil	4 or 5 medium cloves garlic, minced
1 cup minced onion	1 Tbs. dried (or 3 Tbs. minced fresh)
1 lb. spinach, stemmed and minced	basil
about ½ tsp. salt	1 lb. ricotta or cottage cheese
lots of black pepper	2 cups (packed) grated mozzarella
	about ¼ cup grated parmesan

1) Heat the olive oil in a medium-sized skillet. Add onion, and sauté over medium heat until translucent — about 5 minutes.
2) Add spinach, salt, and pepper. Cook, stirring, over high heat for several minutes — until the spinach wilts. Stir in the garlic and basil and cook for about 2 more minutes.
3) Place the cheeses in a medium-sized bowl. Add the spinach sauté and mix very well. Taste to correct seasonings.

TO ASSEMBLE:

1) Preheat oven to 450°F. Oil a baking tray.
2) Punch down the risen dough. Divide it into 6 equal sections, and roll out on a floured surface into circles ¼ inch thick.
3) Place ½ to ¾ cup filling on one half of the circle, leaving a ½-inch rim. Use your fingers or a brush to moisten the rim with a little water. Fold over the empty side and crimp the edges with your favorite fork. Use that same fork to prick little holes here and there on the top surface.
4) Arrange the completed calzones on the oiled tray, and bake for 15 to 20 minutes, or until crisp and lightly browned. OPTIONAL: You can brush each pastry with a little melted butter or some olive oil during the last 5 minutes of baking. Serve hot.

ALTERNATIVE FILLINGS:

- 1 batch Eggplant Scallopini Marsala (p. 83) — it's nondairy.
- 1 batch Asparagus-Mushroom Sauce (p. 77). Replace the butter with olive oil; reduce wine to ½ cup; delete water. (Also nondairy.)
- Thick slices of fresh tomato — with mozzarella and Pesto (p. 84). [If you don't have pesto made, just add a few cloves of sliced garlic, some freshly minced basil, and a drizzle of olive oil.]

SAVORY FILO PASTRIES

40 minutes to prepare;
30 minutes to bake

Yield: 2 rolls (about
6 servings) per recipe

Once you get past the mystique of filo pastry, you will see how easy it is to make delicious, mouthwateringly crisp, savory vegetable strudels. Buy the pastry (sometimes called "Fillo Leaves" or "Greek Phyllo") in a long rectangular package in the frozen foods section of most good grocery stores. Let it thaw out thoroughly while still wrapped (this will take an hour or two). Unwrap just before using, take out a pile of however many sheets you will need, and rewrap (airtight!) and refrigerate the rest until next time. Cover the sheets you are about to use with a slightly damp tea towel — they dry out quickly!

When I first learned to make strudels, I always brushed melted butter between the pastry layers. In recent years, however, I discovered I like using olive oil much better. You don't have to mess around with melting it; it goes further, so you can use much less of it; and it is lighter, has a great flavor, and is cholesterol-free. But if you just love butter so much that it would break your heart to substitute olive oil, try adding some melted butter to the oil, to flavor it. You can also use oil spray.

Broccoli Strudel

- Try making your own bread crumbs by grating some good bread in the food processor. The better-tasting the bread, the better.
- Each of these strudels uses about 10 sheets of filo pastry, which is approximately half a 1-lb. package.

(A little oil, butter, or
  oil spray for the baking tray)
1 Tbs. butter or olive oil
1 cup minced onion
1 large bunch broccoli, finely chopped
½ tsp. salt
lots of black pepper
2 medium cloves garlic, minced

2 cups good bread crumbs
2 cups grated cheddar
2 Tbs. lemon juice (more, to taste)

10 sheets of filo pastry
3 to 4 Tbs. olive oil — OR 6 Tbs.
   melted butter — OR oil spray,
   for the filo

1) Preheat oven to 375°F. Oil a baking tray.

2) Melt butter or heat 1 Tbs. olive oil in a large skillet. Add onion, and sauté for about 5 minutes over medium heat.

3) Add broccoli, salt, and pepper, and cook, stirring, for about 5 more minutes. Add garlic, and sauté until the broccoli is just tender (about 5 more minutes). Remove from heat.

4) Stir in bread crumbs, cheese, and lemon juice. Taste to adjust seasonings.

5) TO ASSEMBLE: Place one sheet of filo on a clean, dry countertop. Brush the top lightly with oil, then add another sheet. Brush with oil, then add another. Continue until you have a pile of 5 leaves. Add half the filling (as illustrated), fold in the sides, and gently roll until you have a neat little log. Brush the top with more oil, then carefully lift the pastry, and place it on the oiled baking sheet. Repeat this procedure to make a second roll, and place it next to the first one on the tray.

filling

6) Bake 25 to 30 minutes, until golden and exquisitely crisp. Cut with a serrated knife, using a gentle sawing motion. Serve hot or at room temperature.

ᴈ ᴈ ᴈ ᴈ ᴈ ᴈ ᴈ ᴈ ᴈ ᴈ

Mushroom Strudel

1 lb. mushrooms, chopped
1 cup (8 oz.) cream cheese or
   cottage cheese (lowfat OK)
1 cup sour cream and/or yogurt
1 tsp. salt
lots of black pepper
1 tsp. dill
1 cup good bread crumbs

2 scallions, finely minced (whites & greens)
¼ cup (packed) minced parsley
3 Tbs. lemon juice
. . . . .
10 sheets of filo pastry
3 to 4 Tbs. olive oil, for the filo
optional: poppy seeds, for the top

1) Preheat oven to 375°F. Oil a baking tray.

2) Place the mushrooms in a saucepan, and cook them all by themselves over medium heat for about 10 minutes. Drain them, squeezing out all the excess liquid, and transfer the mushrooms to a medium-sized bowl. (You can save the discarded liquid for a great soup stock.)

3) Add cream cheese, cut into small pieces, or cottage cheese to the hot mushrooms. Mix well. Stir in remaining filling ingredients.

4) Follow directions in steps 5 and 6 above. A very nice optional touch: sprinkle some poppy seeds on top before baking.

Spanakopita

Heavenly Greek Spinach Pastry

1½ hours
to prepare
and bake

Yield:
about 8
servings

2 Notes ♫: ˢStores well (unbaked) for up to several days. Cover tightly and refrigerate.
ˢDetailed information about filo pastry on p. 162.

(A little oil, butter, or)
(oil spray for the pan)
2 Tbs. olive oil
2 cups minced onion
½ tsp. salt
1 Tbs. dried basil
1 tsp. dried oregano

2½ lbs. fresh spinach, stemmed and finely chopped
5 medium cloves garlic, minced
3 Tbs. flour
2 to 3 cups (packed) crumbled feta cheese (about 1 lb.)
1 cup cottage or pot cheese
black pepper, to taste

⅓ cup olive oil — OR ½ cup melted butter — OR oil spray
1 lb. filo pastry (16 to 20 leaves), thoroughly defrosted

1) Preheat oven to 375°F. Lightly grease a 9 x 13-inch baking pan.
2) Heat the oil in a Dutch oven or deep skillet. Add onion, salt, and herbs, and sauté for about 5 minutes, or until the onion softens. Add the spinach, turn up the heat, and cook, stirring, until the spinach wilts (5 to 8 minutes). Stir in the garlic.
3) Sprinkle in the flour, stir, and cook over medium heat 2 to 3 more minutes. Remove from heat.
4) Mix in the cheeses, then correct the seasonings, adding black pepper to taste along the way.
5) Place a sheet of filo in the prepared pan, letting the pastry edges climb up the sides. Brush it all over with olive oil or melted butter, or spray it with oil spray, then add another sheet. Keep going until you have a stack of 10 oiled or buttered sheets.
6) Add the filling, spreading it evenly to the edges. Continue layering and oiling or buttering the remaining filo on top of the filling. Oil or butter the top layer.
7) Gently (with a serrated knife in a sawing motion) cut the unbaked Spanakopita into squares. Bake uncovered for about 45 minutes, or until golden and crispy. Serve hot or warm.

POLENTA PIE

Easy deep-dish pizza
with a thick and crunchy
cornmeal crust

1¼ hours to prepare
(most of which is
crust-baking time)

Yield:
One 10-inch pie
(serves 4)

FILLING:

CRUST:

1½ cups coarse cornmeal
1 tsp. salt
1½ cups cold water
2 cups boiling water
a little olive oil

1 Tbs. olive oil
1 small onion, thinly sliced
½ cup thinly sliced bell pepper
about 10 mushrooms, sliced
1 small zucchini, thinly sliced
5 to 6 medium cloves garlic, sliced
2 tsp. dried basil (or 2 Tbs. minced fresh basil)
½ tsp. oregano
fresh black pepper
¼ lb. mozzarella cheese, grated
2 small — or 1 medium — ripe tomato(es), sliced

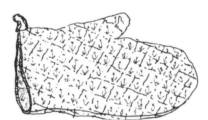

1) Combine cornmeal, salt, and cold water in a small bowl. Have the boiling water on the stove in a saucepan, and add the cornmeal mixture, whisking. Cook about 10 minutes over low heat, stirring frequently. It will get very thick. Remove from heat, and let cool until handleable.

2) Preheat oven to 375°F. Oil a 10-inch pie pan. Add the polenta, and use a spatula and wet hands to form it into a smooth, thick crust over the bottom and sides of the pan. Brush the surface with olive oil, and bake uncovered for 45 minutes.

3) While the crust bakes, heat 1 Tbs. olive oil in a medium-sized skillet. Add the onion, and sauté for 5 to 8 minutes, or until it begins to soften. Add bell pepper, mushrooms, and zucchini, and sauté until everything is tender. Stir in the garlic and herbs, and sauté just a few minutes more.

4) Turn up the oven to broiling temperature. Sprinkle half the cheese onto the bottom of the baked crust, then add the tomato slices. Spread the sautéed mixture over the tomatoes, and sprinkle the remaining cheese on top. Broil until brown (about 5 minutes), and serve hot.

Zucchini-Crusted Pizza

❧❧❧❧❧❧❧❧❧❧❧❧❧❧❧❧❧❧❧❧❧

~ a normal pizza on top, with a beautiful, substantial-yet-tender crust: golden, with flecks of green and a slight crunch.

~ If possible, use a food processor with the grating attachment for the zucchini and mozzarella.

~ You can make the crust up to several days in advance.

❧❧❧❧❧❧❧❧❧❧❧❧❧❧❧❧❧❧❧❧❧❧❧❧❧❧❧❧❧❧❧❧❧❧❧❧❧

olive oil and flour for the pan
2 cups (packed) grated zucchini (about two 7-inchers)
2 eggs, beaten (OK to delete one or both yolks)
¼ cup flour
½ cup grated mozzarella
½ cup grated parmesan
OPTIONAL: pinches of basil, marjoram, and/or rosemary
2 Tbs. olive oil

TOPPING SUGGESTIONS:

extra olive oil
1 large ripe tomato, sliced
extra mozzarella, sliced or grated
2 to 3 large cloves garlic, thinly sliced
sautéed mushrooms
thinly sliced bell peppers
sliced olives

1) Preheat oven to 400°F. Generously oil a 10-inch pie pan and coat lightly with flour. (You can also use a jelly roll pan.)
2) Combine zucchini, eggs, flour, mozzarella, parmesan, herbs, and 1 Tbs. olive oil in a bowl and mix well.
3) Spread into the prepared pan and bake for 35 to 40 minutes, or until golden brown. About halfway through the baking, brush with the remaining tablespoon of olive oil (optional). Remove from oven. When it has cooled for about 10 minutes, use a spatula to loosen the crust from the pan, so it won't break later.
4) Top with your favorite pizza items and bake at 400°F. until heated through.

Eggplant-Almond Enchiladas

... slightly different enchiladas, with deep flavor and wonderful textural contrasts

Serve with rice and plain beans or Refritos (following page). You'll need a batch of Mexican Red Sauce (p.95) made in advance.

1 Tbs. olive oil
1 cup minced onion
6 cups diced eggplant (approximately 1 large or 2 small)
1 tsp. salt (possibly more, to taste)
lots of black pepper
4 medium cloves garlic, minced
1 medium green bell pepper, minced
1 cup lightly toasted almonds, minced
1 packed cup grated jack cheese (or a similar mild white cheese)
12 corn tortillas
1 batch Mexican Red Sauce (p.95)

1) Heat olive oil in a deep skillet or Dutch oven. Add onion, and sauté for about 5 minutes over medium heat.

2) Add eggplant, salt, and pepper, and mix well. Cover and cook for about 10 minutes over medium heat, stirring occasionally, until the eggplant is soft.

3) Add garlic and bell pepper. Stir and cook 5 to 8 more minutes, or until the pepper is just tender. Taste to correct salt.

4) Remove from heat; stir in almonds and cheese.

5) Preheat oven to 350°F. Moisten each tortilla briefly in water, then place approximately ¼ cup of filling on one side and roll up. Gently situate the filled enchiladas in a baking pan. Pour a batch of sauce over the top. Bake uncovered for about 30 minutes.

REFRITOS
(REFRIED BEANS)

ᗡᗡᗡᗡᗡᗡᗡᗡ

The beans need to soak for at least 4 hours; then to cook for about 1¼ hrs. Do other preparations while the beans cook.

Yield:
6 to 8
servings

Serve Refritos in Tostadas (see below) or stuffed into bell peppers and baked, then served over rice with Nachos Sauce (p.94). Or, for a plain and inexpensive dinner, serve with rice, green salad, and warm tortillas.

2 cups dry pinto beans, soaked
2 to 3 Tbs. olive oil
2 cups minced onion
5 to 6 (or even more) medium cloves garlic, minced
2 tsp. cumin
1½ tsp. salt
black pepper
optional: 1 small bell pepper, minced

1) Cook the presoaked beans in plenty of boiling water until very soft. Drain and set aside.

2) Heat the olive oil in a large skillet. Add onion, half the garlic, cumin, and salt. Sauté over medium heat about 10 minutes, or until the onions are soft. Add (or don't add) the optional bell pepper, and sauté another 5 minutes. Add remaining garlic; season with black pepper.

3) Turn heat to low, add beans, and mix well. Mash with a fork or a potato masher, and cook for just a few minutes more. Serve right away, or store in refrigerator or freezer until time to reheat. (Refritos reheat beautifully.)

ᘓᘓᘓᘓᘓᘓᘓᘓᘓ   TOSTADAS   ᗡᗡᗡᗡᗡᗡᗡᗡᗡ

A tostada is a kind of open-faced Mexican sandwich, with many contrasting layers of food piled onto a crispy corn tortilla. Invite your friends over for a tostada-building party. Spread a large table with dishes of tostada components, and do it buffet-style. (Continued →)

Tostada Components:

1) DEEP-FRIED TORTILLAS: Fry corn tortillas in hot oil until crisp. Drain well on paper towels, and serve in a basket.

2) REFRITOS (preceding page)

3) ACCESSORIES: (use all or some ~ or add your own inspired ideas)

shredded lettuce	minced olives	chopped hardboiled egg
finely shredded cabbage	grated cheese	minced mild chilies
Guacamole (p.108)	chopped tomatoes	sour cream

4) HOT SAUCE (p.95) or NACHOS SAUCE (p.94) or SALSA FRESCA (p.96).

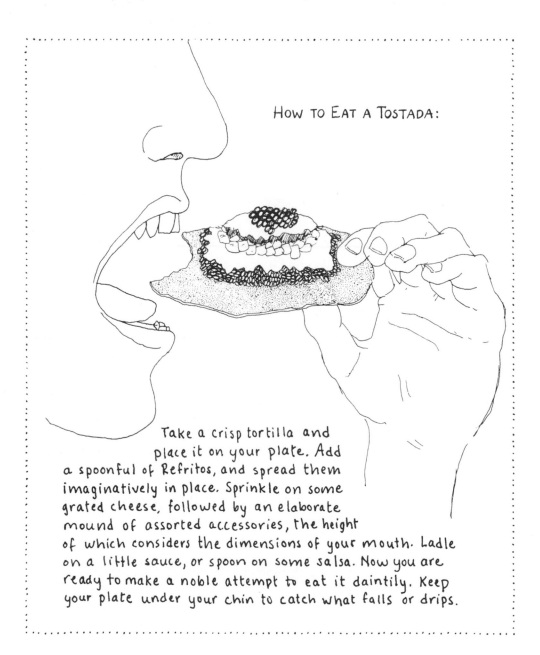

HOW TO EAT A TOSTADA:

Take a crisp tortilla and place it on your plate. Add a spoonful of Refritos, and spread them imaginatively in place. Sprinkle on some grated cheese, followed by an elaborate mound of assorted accessories, the height of which considers the dimensions of your mouth. Ladle on a little sauce, or spoon on some salsa. Now you are ready to make a noble attempt to eat it daintily. Keep your plate under your chin to catch what falls or drips.

SAMOSAS

1½ hours to prepare;
25 minutes to bake

Yield: 15 or 16 medium-sized, very satisfying pastries (enough to feed 6 to 8 people, at least)

Samosas are flaky pastries filled with spicy potatoes and peas. In traditional Indian cuisine, they are deep-fried (and that is still an option). But baking them works very well, and is easier and more healthful.

All components can be made well ahead of time. Finished Samosas can be stored for days in the refrigerator or freezer. Make the Dipping Sauce while the Samosas bake.

Serve Samosas with any curry, or as a simple supper with Gingered Carrot Soup (p.22) and Raita (p.99).

THE DOUGH:

2½ cups flour
½ tsp. salt
1 cup buttermilk or yogurt
extra flour, as needed

1) Place the flour in a medium-sized bowl. Mix in the salt.
2) Make a well in the center, and add the buttermilk or yogurt. Mix first with a spoon and then with your hand, to make a smooth dough.
3) Add extra flour, as needed, to keep the dough from being sticky. The dough will be quite soft. Knead in the bowl for about 5 minutes. Cover tightly and refrigerate until you are ready to assemble the pastries.

THE FILLING:

2 large potatoes (the size of a large person's fist)
1 Tbs. butter
1 cup finely minced onion
2 medium cloves garlic, minced
1 Tbs. freshly grated ginger

1 tsp. mustard seeds
1 tsp. dried coriander (if available)
¾ tsp. salt
1½ cups uncooked green peas (frozen, thawed = fine)
2 Tbs. lemon juice
cayenne, to taste

1) Peel the potatoes and chop them into 1-inch pieces. Place in a saucepan, cover with water, and boil until very soft. Drain and transfer to a medium-sized bowl. Mash and set aside. (continued on next page...)

2) Melt the butter in a heavy skillet. Add onion, garlic, ginger, mustard seeds, coriander, and salt. Sauté over medium heat about 8 to 10 minutes, or until the onions are quite soft. Add this to the mashed potatoes, along with the remaining ingredients. Mix well, but try not to smash the peas. Cool for at least 15 minutes before filling the pastries.

THE DIPPING SAUCE :

½ cup cider vinegar
½ cup water
3 Tbs. brown sugar
1 small clove garlic, minced
1 tsp. salt

1) Place all ingredients in a small saucepan. Stir until the sugar dissolves.
2) Heat to boiling, then let simmer uncovered for about 10 minutes. It will reduce slightly.
3) Serve warm or at room temperature with hot Samosas.

TO ASSEMBLE AND BAKE:

1) Preheat the oven to 425°F. Generously oil a baking sheet.
2) Keep a small container of flour, a fork, a small bowl of water, and a pastry brush close at hand. Flour a clean surface, and, one by one, roll 1-inch balls of dough into 5-inch circles, using a rolling pin.
3) Place approximately 1½ Tbs. filling in the center of each circle, and fold over, just like a turnover. Brush the inside edges of each circle with a little water, and fold the edges together to make a small hem. Crimp the edges firmly with the fork.
   NOTE: If you are storing the Samosas to bake later on, place them on a heavily floured plate or tray, dust the tops with more flour, and cover tightly. Store in the refrigerator or freezer until baking time.
4) To bake: Place the Samosas on the oiled baking sheet. Brush the tops with oil. Bake 15 minutes at 425°F., then reduce heat to 375°F. and bake for 10 minutes more. For maximum crispiness, turn the Samosas over when you turn the oven down.
5) Serve within 15 minutes of baking, with Dipping sauce. A nice way to serve the sauce is in individual saucers or tiny bowls, so each person can hold both Samosa and sauce directly under his or her face while eating, and the sauce bowl can catch the drips. (It does drip, but that's one of the charms of this ritual.)

EGGPLANT CURRY

Preparation time: 45 minutes
(Put up rice when you begin.)

Yield: 6 to 8 servings

2 to 3 Tbs. butter and/or peanut oil
1 Tbs. mustard seeds
2 Tbs. sesame seeds
2 tsp. cumin seeds
1½ cups chopped onion
1½ to 2 tsp. salt
2 tsp. turmeric
¼ tsp. cayenne (possibly more, depending on your tolerance/preference)
2 medium eggplants (7 to 8 inches long; 4-inch diameter at roundest
  point), cut into 1-inch cubes
water, as needed
2 cups frozen or fresh green peas
optional: 1 small bunch fresh cilantro, minced

1) Heat butter or oil over medium heat in a very large, deep skillet or
   Dutch oven. Add seeds, and sauté until they begin to pop (5 minutes).

2) Add onion, salt, turmeric, and cayenne. Cook, stirring occasionally,
   for 8 to 10 minutes, or until the onion is translucent.

3) Add eggplant and salt. Cook, stirring from the bottom regularly,
   for 15 to 20 minutes—until the eggplant is soft. You might need
   to add a little water if the mixture is too dry. Cover the pan
   between stirrings.

4) Steam the peas until they are just tender and bright green. Serve
   the curry over rice, topped with peas and freshly minced cilantro.

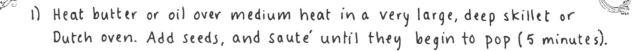

సత్యమ్మ ప్రసిద్ధ గోపి ఉప్పుర కూర
(Satyamma's Famous Cauliflower Curry)

30 to 40 minutes
to prepare

Yield:
about 6 servings

ON THE SIDE

Begin cooking
some rice at
around the
same time you
start preparing
the curry.

2 cups brown
rice in 3 cups
water will be
the right
amount.

2 medium-small (3-inch diameter)
   potatoes, cut into small chunks
½ cup shredded unsweetened coconut
1 Tbs. mustard seeds
3 medium cloves garlic, peeled
1½ Tbs. minced fresh ginger
½ cup lightly toasted peanuts
1 tsp. turmeric
½ tsp. ground cloves or allspice
2 Tbs. toasted cumin seeds
1 to 2 Tbs. toasted sesame seeds
¼ tsp. cayenne
½ cup water (more, as needed)
1 to 2 Tbs. peanut oil
1½ cups chopped onion
1 tsp. salt
1 large cauliflower, cut in 1-inch pieces
1 medium carrot, thinly sliced
optional: 1 cup cooked chick peas
3 to 4 Tbs. lemon juice

ON THE SIDE

Your choice of
   Condiments:

Raita (p.99)
Lemon slices
Orange slices
Toasted Nuts
Toasted Coconut
Raisins
Sliced Cucumbers
Sliced Tomatoes
Thin Strips of
   Bell Pepper
   (assorted colors)

1) Boil the potatoes until just tender. Drain and set aside.

2) Place the next 11 ingredients in a blender and purée until fairly homo-
   genous. Add extra water, as needed, to form a soft, workable paste.

3) Heat the oil in a large, deep skillet or Dutch oven, and add onion and
   salt. Sauté for 5 minutes over medium heat, then add cauliflower and
   carrot and mix well. Cover and cook about 10 minutes, then add the
   paste. Mix well. Cook, covered, over low heat until the cauliflower is
   tender, stirring every few minutes. Add more water, if necessary, to
   prevent sticking.

4) Add the cooked potatoes, chick peas, and lemon juice, and cook a few more
   minutes. Taste to adjust salt, and serve hot, with rice and condiments.

✿ Mushroom Curry ✿

50 minutes to prepare
(put up rice when you
begin)

Yield:
4 to 6
servings

There are a few surprises in this tart-savory-sweet curry. Try sautéing chopped almonds in a little butter or margarine for the topping.

The tomatoes work best if peeled and seeded ahead of time. It's easy: just core them and plunge them into boiling water for 10 seconds. Pull off the peel, then cut them open and squeeze out the seeds. Chop the remaining pulp.

2 Tbs. butter

2 cups chopped onion

3 medium cloves garlic, minced

1 tsp. cumin

1 tsp. cinnamon

1 tsp. turmeric

1 tsp. powdered ginger

1 tsp. mustard seeds

½ tsp. cloves or allspice

1½ tsp. salt (possibly more, to taste)

1 cup chopped celery

1½ lbs. mushrooms, coarsely chopped

3 medium-sized tomatoes, chopped

2 medium-sized tart apples, chopped

½ cup shredded unsweetened coconut

1 Tbs. honey (optional, to taste)

3 to 4 Tbs. lemon juice

cayenne, to taste

optional toppings { yogurt
sautéed or toasted almonds

1) Melt the butter in a large, deep skillet or a Dutch oven. Add onions and garlic, and sauté over medium heat. After a few minutes add spices and salt. Sauté another 5 to 8 minutes ~ until onions are soft.

2) Add celery and mushrooms. Mix well, cover, and simmer another 8 to 10 minutes, stirring occasionally. You can add up to ½ cup water during this time, to prevent sticking. (It makes a nice broth.)

3) When the celery is slightly tender, add tomatoes, apples, coconut, honey, and lemon juice. Cover, and continue to cook until everything is tender, but not mushy. (Additional water may be needed. Use small amounts at a time.) Add cayenne to taste, cover, and let sit for about 10 minutes before serving. Serve over rice.

Yield:
4 or 5
servings

TOMATO CURRY

...delicious on rice, with chutney (p.98) and Raita (p.99) or plain yogurt. Good, also, as an accompaniment to other curries. The eggs go well with the tomatoes, or you can use tofu, which is very similar to the Indian cheese, panir.

PRELIMINARY: Peel and seed the tomatoes beforehand. First, core the tomatoes, and drop them into a saucepanful of boiling water for 10 seconds. Then hold them over a sink and pull off the skins. (They will come right off.) Cut the tomatoes open; squeeze out and discard the seeds. Coarsely chop the remaining pulp.

1 Tbs. butter or oil
1½ cups chopped onion
1 tsp. salt
1 small bell pepper, minced
6 medium-sized ripe tomatoes, peeled and seeded (see above)
2 cups tomato purée
½ tsp. cinnamon
2 tsp. cumin
optional: ½ tsp. ground fenugreek
½ tsp. dried coriander
¼ tsp. cayenne (more, to taste)
optional: 3 hardboiled eggs, peeled and cut into wedges
½ lb. very firm tofu, cut into small cubes
fresh cilantro, minced

2 tsp. mustard seeds
2 tsp grated ginger
3 to 4 medium cloves garlic, minced

1) Melt butter (or heat oil) in a Dutch oven. Add onion, salt, and mustard seeds. Sauté over medium heat for 8 to 10 minutes, or until the onions soften and the seeds begin to pop.
2) Add ginger, garlic, and minced bell pepper, and cook another 5 minutes, or until the pepper begins to be tender.
3) Add remaining ingredients, mix well, and heat just to boiling, stirring frequently. Turn the heat down to a simmer, cover, and cook for 15 to 20 minutes.
4) Serve hot, over rice, with wedges of egg or cubes of tofu artfully arranged on top, and a final sprinkling of minced cilantro.

Preparation time:
about 1¾ hours
after beans are soaked

 Vegetarian Chili

A traditional chili, except with bulgur and without ground meat. Although the concept of "meat substitutes" is hardly compelling, the bulgur really does give a ground-beef-like texture. It also enhances the protein content.

Soak the beans for at least 4 hours (preferably overnight) before cooking. Prepare all other ingredients while the beans are cooking, to save time.

2 ½ cups dry kidney beans, soaked
1 cup tomato juice
1 cup uncooked bulgur wheat
2 Tbs. olive oil
2 cups chopped onion
6 to 8 large cloves garlic, minced
1 medium carrot, diced
1 medium stalk celery, diced
2 tsp. cumin

2 tsp. basil
2 tsp. chili powder (more, to taste)
1½ tsp. salt (more, to taste)
black pepper and cayenne, to taste
1 medium bell pepper, chopped
1 14½-oz. can tomatoes
3 Tbs. tomato paste (half a small can)
finely minced parsley ⎫ optional toppings
grated cheese ⎭

1) Place the soaked beans in a Dutch oven or kettle, cover with water, and bring to a boil. Partially cover, turn heat down to a simmer, and cook until tender (about 1¼ hours). Watch the water level during cooking, adding more if necessary. Drain off any excess water when the beans are done.

2) Heat the tomato juice to boiling. Add it to the bulgur in a small bowl, cover, and let stand 15 minutes. Add this to the cooked beans.

3) Heat the olive oil in a medium-sized skillet. Add onion, half the garlic, carrot, celery, and seasonings. Sauté over medium heat about 5 minutes, add bell pepper, and sauté until all the vegetables are tender.

4) Add the sautéed vegetables, tomatoes (au jus), and tomato paste to the beans. Simmer over lowest possible heat, stirring occasionally, for 20 to 30 minutes or longer. After about 15 minutes, add remaining garlic. Taste to adjust seasonings, and serve hot, topped with parsley and/or cheese.

VEGETABLE STEW

Preparation time:
about 50 minutes

2 Tbs. olive oil and/or butter
3 cups minced onion
3 medium cloves garlic, minced
2 medium potatoes, diced
1 medium (7-inch or so) eggplant, diced
1 tsp. salt (more, to taste)
fresh black pepper, to taste
2 medium stalks celery, chopped
1 healthy stalk broccoli, chopped small
2 to 3 medium carrots, sliced or diced
½ cup dry red wine (optional)
2 small (6-inch) zucchini, diced
3 Tbs. (half a small can) tomato paste
½ lb. mushrooms, coarsely chopped
3 Tbs. molasses
2 tsp. dill
sour cream or yogurt } optional
finely minced parsley } toppings

Yield:
about 6 servings

1) Heat oil (or melt butter) in a Dutch oven. Add onion, garlic, potatoes, eggplant, salt, and pepper. Cover and cook over medium heat, stirring often, until the potatoes are tender. Add small amounts of water, as needed, to prevent sticking.

2) Add celery, broccoli, and carrots, along with optional red wine. Continue to cook over medium heat, covered but occasionally stirring, until all the vegetables begin to be tender (8 to 10 minutes).

3) Add remaining ingredients (except toppings) and stir. Cover and simmer very quietly about 15 minutes more, stirring every once in a while. Taste to correct seasonings.

Serve piping hot, topped
with sour cream or yogurt
and minced parsley.

Polenta

Cornmeal mush with Class

For a super-easy, super-fast meal, serve Polenta in a bowl topped with a little olive oil or butter and some cheese. Or top it with Pesto (p. 84), Gorgonzola (or any blue cheese), chopped fresh tomatoes, and a generous amount of coarsely ground black pepper. You can also serve Polenta under or next to Ratatouille or its Spicy Variation (see following page) or paired with any kind of chili or bean dish (see pages 176 and 134).

> 5 cups water
> 1½ cups coarse cornmeal
> ½ tsp. salt
> OPTIONAL TOPPINGS : See above

1) Place 4 cups of water in a medium-sized saucepan and bring to a boil.

2) Combine the cornmeal with the remaining cup of water in a small bowl, and mix until uniform.

3) Spoon the cornmeal mixture into the boiling water, add salt, and whisk until smooth.

4) Turn the heat down to a simmer, and cook, stirring often, for about 10 minutes, or until very thick.

Ratatouille

Preparation time:
about 45 minutes

Yield:
4 to 6 servings

Mediterranean vegetable stew

3 Tbs. olive oil
4 medium cloves garlic
2 cups chopped onion
1 bay leaf
1 medium eggplant (7 to
   8 inches long; 4 to 5-inch
   diameter), cubed
1½ tsp. salt
1½ tsp. basil
1 tsp. marjoram or oregano
½ tsp. rosemary
½ tsp. thyme
1 medium (6- to 7-inch)
   zucchini, cubed

2 medium bell peppers, in strips
fresh black pepper
1 14½-oz. can tomatoes
freshly minced parsley } optional
minced olives

FOR SPICY VARIATION:
- omit bay leaf, marjoram, rosemary,
- add in their place:
   1½ tsp. cumin
   2 tsp. chili powder
   cayenne, to taste
- (optional): add 1 cup pitted,
   sliced oil-cured olives

1) Heat olive oil in a deep skillet or Dutch oven. Add garlic, onion, and bay leaf, and sauté over medium heat for about 5 minutes.

2) Add eggplant, salt, and herbs, and stir. Cover and cook over medium heat, stirring occasionally, for 15 to 20 minutes, or until the eggplant is soft.

3) Add zucchini, bell peppers, black pepper, and tomatoes. (Break the tomatoes into smaller pieces with a spoon.) Cover and simmer for about 10 more minutes, or until the zucchini and bell peppers are tender.

4) Serve hot, warm, or at room temperature — plain, or topped with parsley and/or olives.

Gado Gado

Preparation time: about 1 hour
(Much of this can be made
in advance.)

Yield: approximately
6 servings

An Indonesian extravaganza: Yellow rice on a bed of spinach, covered with vegetables, tofu, and hardboiled eggs. A gingery peanut sauce gets drizzled over the top, and crunchy, flavorful "final toppings" add a delightful finishing touch. AND IT'S ALL QUITE EASY - EVEN FOR BEGINNERS! HAVE FUN WITH THIS!

NOTE: All the ingredients can be prepared in advance and served warm or at room temperature.

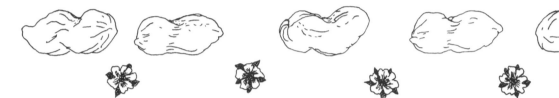

GADO-GADO:

NOTE: You can vary the vegetables and their amounts. Also, they can be cooked or raw - or some of each. Arrange everything on a platter or on individual plates.

1) A bed of <u>fresh spinach</u> goes on the bottom.

2) <u>Yellow rice</u> goes on the spinach. (To make yellow rice, cook 2 cups rice in 3 cups simmering water with ½ tsp. turmeric. Add a little extra water toward the end of the cooking, if needed.) until tender.

3) <u>An assortment of vegetables</u> goes on the rice. Such as:
   ~ A small bunch of broccoli, cut into small spears and steamed
   ~ Fresh green beans, lightly steamed
   ~ Red and green cabbage, very finely shredded
   ~ Thin slices of carrot, lightly steamed or raw
   ~ Mung bean sprouts

4) <u>Tofu and hardboiled eggs</u> (sliced or chopped) go on the vegetables.

PEANUT SAUCE:

1 cup creamy peanut butter	4 Tbs. cider vinegar
1 heaping Tbs. grated ginger	2 Tbs. soy sauce
1 heaping Tbs. minced garlic	1 tsp. salt (possibly more, if
3 Tbs. brown sugar	peanut butter is unsalted)
1½ cups hot water	Crushed red pepper, to taste

1) Put everything in a blender and purée until smooth. If it's too thick, add a little extra water.
2) Transfer to a serving bowl and adjust seasonings to taste. Serve at any temperature, drizzled over Gado Gado. (This makes about 2 cups sauce.)

FINAL TOPPINGS:

3 Tbs. peanut or canola oil
2 Tbs. sliced fresh ginger (<u>very</u> thin slices, done
    with your sharpest paring knife)
1 cup finely minced onion
12 medium cloves garlic, peeled and thinly sliced

OPTIONAL
{
Shredded, unsweetened coconut, lightly toasted
Crushed red pepper
Slices of fruit:
    lemons, limes, oranges, apples, pineapple
}

1) Heat 1 Tbs. oil in a small skillet. Add ginger, and sauté over medium heat for a minute or so, then transfer to a small bowl.
2) Repeat with the onion and garlic, sautéing each separately in 1 Tbs. oil for 8 to 10 minutes (onion) and about 20 seconds (garlic). Place each in a small bowl.
3) Place some or all of these toppings on the table with the Gado Gado, so each person can liberally garnish his or her own portion.

Preparation time = 30 minutes, plus at least 2 hours to marinate. Actual cooking time is about 10 to 15 minutes.

VEGETABLE KEBABS

Serves 6
(2 skewers apiece)

MARINADE: (can be doubled, if you like lots of extra for basting)
2/3 cup olive oil
1/4 cup red wine vinegar
5 medium cloves garlic, minced
1/2 tsp. salt
lots of freshly ground black pepper

1/2 tsp. marjoram or oregano
1/2 tsp. thyme
1/2 tsp. basil
a pinch or two of rosemary

1 medium (6-to 7-inch long) eggplant, cut into 1 1/2-inch cubes
about a dozen cherry tomatoes
about a dozen medium-sized mushrooms
1 or 2 bell peppers (any color), cut into 2-inch strips
1 medium onion, cut into 1 1/2-inch wedges
1 1/2 lbs. very firm tofu, cut into 1 1/2-inch cubes
OPTIONAL ADDITIONS:
1-inch slices of corn-on-the-cob, parboiled 5 minutes
1 1/2-inch chunks of potato or sweet potato, parboiled about 8 minutes
    (until just tender)
1-inch chunks of zucchini or any summer squash

1) Prepare marinade in a long, shallow baking pan.
2) Add all other ingredients and stir gently. Let marinate, stirring occasion-ally, for at least 2 hours, and as long as overnight. (You don't have to get up and stir in the middle of the night.)
3) Arrange the marinated tidbits on 9- or 10-inch skewers in an imagi-native sequence. Grill over hot coals or broil, basting frequently with the marinade and turning every few minutes. The cooking time is not exact, so watch them carefully, and remove from the heat as soon as they seem done (tender, browned, perfect). Baste one more time, and serve hot to your delighted guests, not forgetting to mention that the skewers, if metal, might be hot. Serve with rice or pasta.

Szechwan Eggplant & Tofu

Most of the preparation for this deeply seasoned stir-fry can be done well ahead of time. In addition, put up some rice to cook about 30 to 40 minutes before beginning the stir-fry.

3 Tbs. soy sauce
¼ cup dry sherry or Chinese rice wine
1 Tbs. white or brown sugar
1 Tbs. cider vinegar
3 Tbs. cornstarch

2 Tbs. peanut oil
1 medium onion, thinly sliced
1 large eggplant, cut into strips
  (thin slices lengthwise, then
  cut across. This should make
  about 7 to 8 cups of strips.)

¾ tsp. salt
2 Tbs. minced garlic
1 Tbs. minced fresh ginger
¼ tsp. black pepper

cayenne pepper, to taste
3 cakes (about ¾ lb.) firm tofu, cut into strips
8 scallions: greens minced, whites in strips (keep separate)
1 medium bunch fresh cilantro, minced (optional)

1) Combine soy sauce, sherry, sugar, and vinegar in a liquid-measuring cup. Add enough water to make 1 cup. Place cornstarch in a small bowl, pour in the liquid, and whisk until dissolved. Set aside, keeping the whisk handy.

2) Heat a large wok over a high flame. Add oil and onion, and stir-fry for about a minute. Add eggplant and salt, and stir-fry for 8 to 10 minutes, until the eggplant is soft. Add garlic, ginger, black pepper, and cayenne. Cook a few minutes more.

3) Add tofu and scallion bottoms. Stir the bowl of liquid (step 1) from the bottom, using the whisk, and add to the wok. Mix well, and stir-fry another few minutes, until the sauce is thick.

4) Remove from heat, and serve over rice, topped with minced scallion greens and fresh cilantro.

Carrot-Mushroom Loaf

30 minutes to assemble;
45 minutes to bake

Yield: 6 to 8 servings

I don't know why this is called a loaf, since it is baked in a 9 x 13-inch pan. But it's been called a loaf for so long, I hate to tamper with tradition. It's a hard dish to stop eating, especially if it comes out of the oven when everyone is hungry.

A food processor fitted with the grating attachment makes short work of this casserole. Use it first to make the bread crumbs, then to grate both the carrots and the cheese — without cleaning it in between.

You can use store-bought bread crumbs, but homemade ones will make this dish taste exceptional. To make superb bread crumbs, the trick is to use superb bread.

NOTE: Once baked, this casserole can be frozen. It reheats beautifully.

2 cups minced onion	3 to 4 medium cloves garlic, minced
1 Tbs. butter	1½ lbs. carrots, grated (about 6 cups)
1 lb. mushrooms, chopped	2 cups superb bread crumbs
1½ tsp. salt	1 cup (packed) grated cheddar
1 tsp. basil	2 eggs, beaten
1 tsp. thyme	black pepper, to taste
1 tsp. dill	OPTIONAL TOPPINGS: extra dill, cheese, bread crumbs; a sprinkling of sesame seeds } any, some, or all (ALL = GREAT!)

1) Lightly oil a 9 x 13-inch baking pan. Preheat the oven to 350°F.

2) In a large skillet, sauté onions in butter over medium heat for about 5 minutes. Add mushrooms, salt, herbs, and garlic, and continue to sauté for about 10 more minutes.

3) In a large bowl, combine carrots, bread crumbs, cheese, eggs, and pepper. Add the sautéed mixture and mix well. Spread into the prepared pan and sprinkle with your choice of toppings. Cover the pan with foil.

4) Bake for 30 minutes covered, then uncover and bake 15 minutes more. Serve hot or warm.

DESSERTS

CONTENTS: DESSERTS

Date-Nut Cake

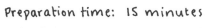

Preparation time: 15 minutes
Baking time: 40 to 50 minutes

Yield: about 6 servings

butter and flour for the pan
3 eggs, separated and
  at room temperature
1/4 cup sugar
1/2 tsp. vanilla extract

1/3 cup flour
1/4 tsp. salt
3/4 cup very finely chopped
  nuts (walnuts, almonds, or pecans)
1 cup chopped dates

TOPPING
1/2 pint heavy cream or 1 cup ricotta cheese
1/2 tsp. vanilla extract
2 to 3 Tbs. powdered sugar (or, to taste)

1) Preheat oven to 350°F. Generously butter and flour a 9-inch round pan.

2) In a medium-sized bowl, beat the egg whites with an electric mixer at high speed until stiff but not dry.

3) In a second medium-sized bowl, beat the egg yolks with sugar and vanilla for several minutes — until smooth and thick.

4) Stir the flour, salt, nuts, and dates into the yolk mixture and blend well. Gently fold in the beaten egg whites.

5) Transfer to the prepared pan and bake for 40 minutes, or until the surface of the cake springs back when touched lightly. Remove from the oven and allow to cool in the pan. Invert onto a serving plate.

6) Combine the cream or ricotta with vanilla and powdered sugar, and whip to your favorite consistency. Spread over the top of the cake, and chill. Serve cold.

Orange Cake

Preparation time: 30 minutes
Baking time: 50 to 60 minutes
~Allow time to cool and glaze.

Yield: 1 large cake,
serves 12 to 16

butter for the pan
1½ cups (3 sticks) butter, softened
1¾ cups sugar
4 eggs

1 tsp. grated orange rind
1 tsp. vanilla extract
3 cups flour
1 Tbs. baking soda

½ tsp. salt
1 cup sour cream or yogurt
½ cup orange juice } whisked together

ORANGE GLAZE:
½ cup orange juice
1 to 2 Tbs. sugar
1 Tbs. lemon juice
optional: 2 to 3 Tbs. dry sherry or orange liqueur

1) Preheat oven to 350°F. Butter a 10-inch tube or bundt pan.
2) In a large bowl, beat together the butter and sugar until light and fluffy.
3) Add the eggs, one at a time, beating well after each.
4) Stir in the orange rind and vanilla. Set aside.
5) Sift together the dry ingredients in a separate bowl. Add this to the butter mixture alternately with the combined sour cream (or yogurt) and orange juice, beginning and ending with the dry ingredients. Mix by hand after each addition—just enough to combine well.
6) Turn into the prepared pan. Bake 50 to 60 minutes, or until a knife inserted all the way down comes out clean. Cool for about 15 minutes, then invert onto a plate. Allow to cool completely.
7) Combine the glaze ingredients in a small saucepan and bring to a boil. Lower heat and simmer uncovered for about 3 minutes. Pour the hot glaze onto the cooled cake. Let stand at least 10 minutes before slicing.

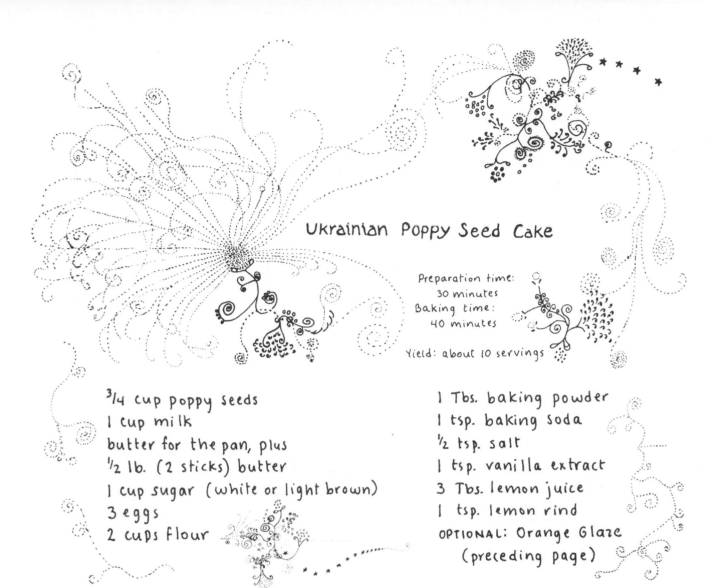

Ukrainian Poppy Seed Cake

Preparation time:
30 minutes
Baking time:
40 minutes

Yield: about 10 servings

¾ cup poppy seeds
1 cup milk
butter for the pan, plus
½ lb. (2 sticks) butter
1 cup sugar (white or light brown)
3 eggs
2 cups flour

1 Tbs. baking powder
1 tsp. baking soda
½ tsp. salt
1 tsp. vanilla extract
3 Tbs. lemon juice
1 tsp. lemon rind
OPTIONAL: Orange Glaze
(preceding page)

1) Place poppy seeds and milk in a small saucepan. Heat just to the boiling point, but remove from heat before it actually boils. (This is called scalding.) Set aside and allow to cool for at least 15 minutes.

2) Preheat oven to 350°F. Butter a 10-inch tube or bundt pan.

3) Cream the butter and sugar in a large mixing bowl. Add eggs, one at a time, beating well after each.

4) Sift together the dry ingredients in a separate bowl. Add this to the butter mixture alternately with the poppy seed-milk, beginning and ending with the dry mixture. Stir just enough to blend thoroughly, adding the vanilla, lemon juice, and lemon rind at the end.

5) Spread the batter into the prepared pan, and bake for about 40 minutes, or until a cake tester comes out clean. Cool for 10 minutes, then invert onto a plate. Allow to cool completely before adding the Orange Glaze (same method as on preceding page) and/or slicing.

Pound Cake

Preparation time:
15 minutes

Baking time: 50
to 60 minutes

Yield:
12 to 16
servings

The most basic cake – and the most buttery. Try it plain for dessert, or topped with fresh Fruit Salad (p. 54) for a serious snack. You can also slice it thinly and toast it for tea or brunch. A few variations appear on the opposite page, and you can explore even further with your own ideas.

butter and flour for the pans
1 lb. (4 sticks) butter, softened
3 cups sugar
6 eggs
4 cups flour
1 Tbs. baking powder
½ tsp. salt
1 cup milk
2 tsp. vanilla extract

1) Preheat oven to 350°F. Butter and flour the bottom and sides of a 10-inch tube or bundt pan.

2) In a large bowl, cream together butter and sugar with an electric mixer at high speed until light and fluffy.

3) Add eggs, one at a time, beating well after each. Set aside.

4) Sift together the dry ingredients in a separate bowl. Mix together the milk and vanilla. Add dry and wet alternately to butter mixture, beginning and ending with dry. Mix by hand – just enough to blend thoroughly without excess beating.

5) Spread the batter into the prepared pan. Bake 50 to 60 minutes, or until a sharp knife inserted all the way down comes out clean. Allow to cool for 10 minutes in the pan, then turn out onto a plate. Cool completely before slicing.

Pound Cake Variations

Here are some delightful adulterations you can perform in your own kitchen. For each of these variations, follow the pound cake recipe on the opposite page, with the following changes:

Lemon Pound Cake

1) Replace vanilla with lemon extract.

2) Add ¼ cup fresh lemon juice.

3) Add 1 tsp. freshly grated lemon rind.

Blueberry Pound Cake

~ Same changes as for Lemon Pound Cake, plus:
2 cups fresh blueberries, folded in gently with the last addition of dry ingredients

Mocha-Swirl Pound Cake

1) Replace the milk with 1 cup strong black coffee.

2) After the batter is all assembled, transfer about ⅓ of it to a small bowl, and add 1 oz. (1 square) melted unsweetened chocolate. Mix thoroughly.

3) Spread the plain batter into the prepared pan and spoon clumps of chocolate batter on top. Using a humble dinner knife, cut through to the bottom of the pan and swirl the dark and light together to create a marbled effect. Bake as directed.

Carrot Cake

butter, or oil for the pan(s)
optional: about ¼ cup poppy seeds

1½ cups (3 sticks) butter, softened
1¾ cups (packed) brown sugar
4 eggs
3 tsp. vanilla extract
1 tsp. grated lemon rind
4 cups flour
1 tsp. salt
½ tsp. baking soda
1 Tbs. baking powder
1 tsp. allspice
2 tsp. cinnamon
2½ cups (packed) finely shredded carrot } combined
¼ cup lemon juice

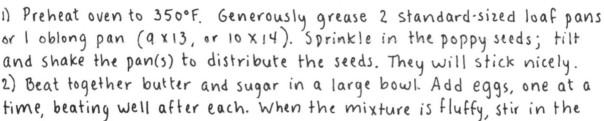

OPTIONAL ADDITIONS: ¾ cup raisins or currants
¾ cup chopped pecans or walnuts
½ cup shredded unsweetened coconut

1) Preheat oven to 350°F. Generously grease 2 standard-sized loaf pans or 1 oblong pan (9 x 13, or 10 x 14). Sprinkle in the poppy seeds; tilt and shake the pan(s) to distribute the seeds. They will stick nicely.
2) Beat together butter and sugar in a large bowl. Add eggs, one at a time, beating well after each. When the mixture is fluffy, stir in the vanilla and lemon rind.
3) Sift together the dry ingredients. Add this to the butter mixture alternately with the carrots, beginning and ending with the dry mixture. Mix just enough after each addition to combine — don't overmix. Stir in the optional items (or not) with the last flour addition.
4) Spread the batter evenly in the pan(s), and bake 40 to 50 minutes (loaf pans) or 35 minutes (oblong pan) — or until a probe inserted into the center comes out clean. For loaf pans: cool 10 minutes in the pan, then rap the pan sharply, and dislodge and remove the cake. Transfer to a rack, and let it cool at least 1 hour before slicing.

Banana Bread

Banana Bread is basically the same recipe as Carrot Cake (opposite page), but with the following changes:

1) Replace the poppy seeds with sesame seeds.

2) Use 2½ tsp. vanilla extract and ½ tsp. almond extract.

3) Use orange rind, instead of lemon.

4) Substitute ½ tsp. nutmeg for the allspice.

5) Replace the carrot with 2 cups puréed ripe banana soaked in 1 cup strong black coffee (can be decaf).

6) Omit the raisin/currant and coconut options.

Apricot-Almond Bread

40 minutes to prepare;
about 1 1/2 hours to bake

Yield: 1 large loaf

Moist and tart with apricots and crunchy with almonds, this bread is ideal for brunches and teas. It's also good as a mid-evening semi-dessert, when you want Something — sweet, but not too — and you don't know exactly what. Try this bread at such times.

butter for the pan	1 tsp. salt
1 1/2 cups thinly sliced dried apricots	2 Tbs. softened butter
1 1/2 cups water	1/2 cup honey or real maple syrup
2 1/2 cups flour	1 egg, beaten
1 tsp. baking soda	1 tsp. vanilla extract
2 tsp. baking powder	1/2 to 1 tsp. orange rind
	1 cup finely chopped almonds

1) Preheat oven to 350°F. Butter a large loaf pan.
2) Place apricots and water in a medium-sized saucepan and bring to a boil. Lower the heat, cover, and simmer for 10 minutes. Transfer to a medium-sized bowl, and allow to cool for about 15 minutes.
3) Sift together dry ingredients (except almonds) in a separate bowl.
4) Stir the butter plus honey or syrup into the cooled apricot mixture. Beat in the egg and vanilla.
5) Add the dry ingredients, orange rind, and almonds. Mix minimally but well.
6) Spread into the prepared pan, and bake about 1 1/2 hours, or until a probe inserted all the way down comes out clean. Let cool for 10 minutes in the pan, then rap the pan firmly a few times on its sides and bottom. The bread should slip right out. Cool at least 15 minutes more before attempting to slice.

Cardamom Coffee Cake

2 1/2 hours, beginning to end

Use a large tube pan – 10 x 4"; 16-cup capacity. This is a large cake!

16 servings

Oil or butter for the pan
1 lb. (4 sticks) butter, softened
2 cups (packed) light brown sugar
4 eggs
2 tsp. vanilla extract
4 cups flour
2 tsp. baking powder
2 1/2 tsp. baking soda

1/2 tsp. salt
1 Tbs. ground cardamom
2 cups sour cream, yogurt, or buttermilk

combine {
NUT MIXTURE:
1/4 cup (packed) light brown sugar
1 Tbs. cinnamon
1/2 cup minced walnuts
}

1) Preheat the oven to 325°F. Grease a large tube pan (see note above).

2) In a large bowl, beat the butter and sugar together until light and fluffy. Add the eggs, one at a time, beating well after each. Stir in the vanilla.

3) Sift the dry ingredients (not including the nut mixture) into a second bowl. Add 1/3 of this at a time to the butter mixture, alternating with the sour cream/yogurt/buttermilk. Stir just enough to blend after each addition.

4) Spoon approximately 1/3 of the batter into the prepared pan, and sprinkle it with half the nut mixture. Add another 1/3 of the batter, followed by the remaining nut mixture and then the rest of the batter. Spread lightly in place.

5) Bake for approximately 1 1/2 hours (possibly longer) until a knife inserted all the way in comes out clean. Cool in the pan for about 20 minutes, then remove the tube-plus-cake from the rim, and let the cake cool completely. Use a sharp knife to loosen the cake, then invert onto a plate and serve.

🍎 APPLE STRUDEL 🍎

This delicious and straightforward Apple Strudel can be made several days in advance and stored, unbaked, in the refrigerator (tightly wrapped Baked strudel also keeps very well in the refrigerator or freezer if wrap airtight. If you freeze it, defrost it completely before reheating it, uncover in a 350°F oven for about 20 minutes —or until crispened.

NOTE: To make fine bread crumbs, cut several thick slices of whole wheat or white bread, and let them dry out for a few hours. Then toast the slices lightly, and grind them to a fine meal in a blender or a food processor.

6 Tbs. vegetable oil —OR ½ cup melted butter —OR oil spray
1½ lbs. tart apples (about 8 medium ones), peeled and chopped
¼ cup sugar
A pinch of salt
1 tsp. cinnamon
3 Tbs. fresh lemon juice

1 Tbs. grated lemon rind
½ cup minced walnuts, lightly toasted
½ cup fine bread crumbs
¼ cup raisins (optional)
1 cup grated cheddar (optional)
A 1-lb. package filo pastry

1) Preheat oven to 375°F. Brush a baking tray with a little of the oil or melted butter, or spray it with oil spray. (Save most of the oil or butter for the filo.)

2) Place all the ingredients except the filo in a large bowl, and toss gently until everything is evenly distributed.

3) Place a sheet of filo on a clean, dry surface, and brush it lightly all over with oil or melted butter —or spray it with oil spray. Lay another sheet on top, oil or butter it all over, and continue until you have a pile of 6. Distribute ⅓ of the apple mixture here ⌐▢┘, fold over the sides ▢, and roll up ▢ this way.

4) Oil or butter the top of the roll, then transfer it to the prepared tray. Repeat with the remaining ingredients to make 2 more rolls.

5) Bake for about 35 minutes, or until lightly browned and exquisitely crisp. Serve warm or at room temperature.

⌘⌘ MERINGUES ⌘⌘

These two versions provide a contrast of textures: an ethereal crunch on the first bite, followed by full-bodied chewiness. The baking process is slow and gradual — almost more of a drying-out than an actual baking.

TO BAKE MERINGUES: Preheat oven to 250°F. Lightly grease a baking tray OR line it with parchment or waxed paper. Bake the meringues for 2½ to 3 hours without opening the oven. Then turn off the oven, and leave them in there for at least 15 minutes. (You can also leave them in for up to an hour or two. This part is flexible!) Cool completely before removing them from the tray.

Meringues will turn out softer or firmer, depending on the humidity in your kitchen. Store them in an airtight bin lined with waxed paper.

ONE MORE THING: Separate the eggs while they're cold, then let the whites come to room temperature.

---

10 minutes to prepare ⌘ CHOCOLATE MERINGUES ⌘ Yield: 1½ dozen
3 hours to bake   (easily doubled)

1 cup powdered sugar	OPTIONAL:	4 egg whites
2 Tbs. cocoa	¼ cup hazelnuts,	½ tsp. vanilla
a pinch of salt	pecans, or almonds	optional: ½ cup chocolate chips

1) Sift together powdered sugar, cocoa, and salt. If you're adding nuts, place them in a blender or food processor with the sugar mixture, and grind in a series of spurts until the nuts and sugar form a fine powder.
2) Beat together the egg whites and vanilla at high speed until they form stiff peaks. Fold in the sugar-nut mixture (or just the cocoa-sugar) and the chocolate chips.
3) Drop by rounded tablespoonfuls onto the prepared tray. Bake as described above.

---

15 minutes to prepare; ⌘ LEMON MERINGUES ⌘ Yield: 1 dozen
3 hours to bake   (easily doubled)

	¼ cup fresh lemon juice	
2 Tbs. cornstarch	¼ cup water	3 egg whites
½ cup powdered sugar	½ tsp. grated lemon rind	1 Tbs. granulated sugar

1) Place cornstarch and powdered sugar in a small saucepan.
2) Combine the lemon juice and water, and whisk this into the cornstarch-sugar. Stir in the lemon rind.
3) Heat to boiling, whisking frequently. Lower heat to a simmer; cook and whisk until very thick. (This will only take about a minute.) Cool for 15 minutes.
4) Beat the egg whites at medium speed until they get foamy. Add the granulated sugar, then beat at high speed until the egg whites form stiff peaks.
5) Add the lemon mixture, and fold until fairly well mixed. (It won't be uniform.) Drop by rounded tablespoons onto the prepared tray. Bake as described above.

Preparation time:
1½ hours – most of
which is for
simmering

STOVETOP RICE PUDDING
~ Eggless, and possibly even dairy-free!

To make this recipe with leftover cooked rice: place 2 cups cooked rice in a saucepan with 1 cup milk. Heat to boiling, lower heat to a simmer, and cook, covered, for 20 to 30 minutes, or until the milk is mostly absorbed. Add remaining ingredients and mix well.

1 cup short-grain brown rice
3 to 3½ cups milk (low-or nonfat, rice, or soy)
½ to ¾ tsp. salt
3 to 5 Tbs. sugar, honey, or real maple syrup
½ tsp. vanilla extract

½ tsp. cinnamon
a dash of nutmeg
a handful of raisins ⎱
2 to 3 tsp. lemon juice ⎰ OPTIONAL
extra cinnamon or
          nutmeg

possible toppings: yogurt
chopped fresh or dried fruit
chopped nuts

1) Rinse the rice in a strainer. Drain well, and place in a saucepan with 3 cups milk. Bring to a boil, cover, and lower heat as much as possible. Simmer until the rice is very tender. This will take up to 1½ hours.

2) About 1 hour into the cooking, stir in salt, sweetening, vanilla, spices, and optional raisins. (When adding the sweetening, start with about 3 Tbs. This dish is naturally sweet, and it's easy to overdo it.)

3) Optional Step: If you want an extra-thick and creamy rice pudding, purée about 1 cup of the rice in a blender with ½ cup additional milk. Return the purée to the rest of the rice; mix well.

4) Stir in lemon juice to taste, if desired, and adjust sweetening. Optional: sprinkle a little extra cinnamon and/or nutmeg on top (go easy!) for a finishing touch. Serve at room temperature or cold, possibly topped with yogurt, fresh or dried fruit, and/or nuts.

old-fashioned
BREAD PUDDING

Humble and easy, yet very rewarding. And transcendent served warm, with ice cream!

This is one of the few instances where ordinary white bread is actually preferable to whole grain.

3 to 4 packed cups cubed bread
  (OK if stale or frozen)
3 eggs
3 cups milk (lowfat OK)
⅓ cup sugar (more or less, to taste)
½ tsp. salt
2 tsp. vanilla extract

OPTIONAL TOPPINGS:
- ice cream
- Berry Sauce (p. 207)
- sliced fresh peaches and/or strawberries

1) Preheat oven to 350°F. Have ready a 9 x 13-inch baking pan.
2) Spread the bread in the pan.
3) Beat together remaining ingredients. Pour this custard over the bread.
4) Bake about 35 minutes, or until firm but not dry. Serve warm or at room temperature.

VARIATIONS

POOR PERSON'S TRIFLE

add to custard:
- ¼ cup rum
- 1½ cups crushed pineapple au jus (canned-in-juice = fine)
- 1½ cups berries or pitted cherries (frozen unsweetened = fine. No need to defrost.)
- OPTIONAL: 1 cup chopped walnuts

BREAD & CHOCOLATE PUDDING

Add to the bread: 1½ cups semisweet chocolate chips

BANANA BREAD PUDDING

Add to the bread: 1 or 2 ripe bananas, sliced.
OPTIONAL: a few dashes of cinnamon and nutmeg.

⎯ Baked Custard ⎯
(Bittersweet Chocolate; Maple; Maple-Peach)

Easy super-comfort food

Yield: 6
custard cups

BITTERSWEET CHOCOLATE CUSTARD:

Preparation time:
20 minutes
(45 minutes to bake)

2½ cups milk (lowfat works just fine)
¾ to 1 cup semisweet chocolate chips (depending
on how deeply chocophilic you are)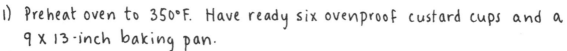
4 eggs
½ tsp. salt
1 tsp. vanilla extract

1) Preheat oven to 350°F. Have ready six ovenproof custard cups and a
9 X 13-inch baking pan.
2) Place the milk and chocolate chips in a small saucepan. Heat gently,
stirring occasionally, until all the chips are melted. Remove from heat
and stir until blended. Allow to cool for about 15 minutes.
3) Place remaining ingredients in a blender or food processor. Add the milk
mixture, scraping in all the wayward clumps of chocolate, and whip
until frothy.
4) Divide the batter among the custard cups. Place them in the baking
pan, and half-fill it with water. Bake 40 to 45 minutes, or until the
custards are solid in the center when shaken.
5) Carefully remove the cups from the baking pan. Cool to room temperature,
then cover each one tightly with plastic wrap and chill.

MAPLE CUSTARD

Preparation time:
10 minutes

omit chocolate chips
add ⅓ cup real maple syrup
optional: a dash each of cinnamon and nutmeg

~ Skip Step 2. Blend all ingredients together in Step 3. Bake as directed.

MAPLE-PEACH CUSTARD

Preparation time:
15 minutes

1½ to 2 cups sliced fresh peaches

~ Make Maple Custard batter. Divide the peaches among the custard cups,
pour the custard over the peaches, and bake as directed.

STRAWBERRY·RHUBARB CRISP

...An easy cobbler with a very crunchy top. Use the smaller amount of sugar if you like it tart. It would be a good idea to have some vanilla ice cream on hand, since you might decide that you can't bear not to have this dessert à la mode.

2 lbs. fresh rhubarb,
   cut into 1-inch chunks
3 to 4 cups sliced strawberries
1/3 to 1/2 cup white sugar

1 1/4 cups rolled oats
1 cup flour
1/4 cup brown sugar
3/4 tsp. cinnamon
a dash or two of both
   allspice and nutmeg
1/2 tsp. salt
1/2 cup (1 stick) melted butter

1) Preheat oven to 375°F.
2) Combine the rhubarb and strawberries in a 9-inch square pan. Sprinkle with white sugar.
3) Mix together the remaining ingredients in a medium-sized bowl. Distribute over the top of the fruit and pat firmly into place.
4) Bake uncovered for 35 to 40 minutes, or until the top is crisp and lightly browned and the fruit is bubbling around the edges. Serve hot, warm, or at room temperature, plain or à la mode.

variations using other fruits:
APPLE CRISP
• Use 6 to 8 cups peeled and sliced tart apples
• 2 to 3 Tbs. lemon juice
• 1/4 cup white sugar
• increase cinnamon (use up to 1 tsp.)
• optional: add 1/2 cup finely chopped walnuts to the topping

PEACH (or APRICOT) - CHERRY CRISP
• Use about 4 cups peeled and sliced peaches or apricots, plus
   2 cups pitted, halved dark cherries (OK to use frozen unsweetened)
• Same adjustments as in Apple Crisp. In addition, you can increase the
   nutmeg to 1/4 tsp. and use almonds instead of walnuts in the topping.

Apple
Custard
Pie

Preparation time: 25 minutes

Baking time: 45 minutes

Yield: 4 to 6 servings

2 cups peeled and thinly sliced tart apples

1 unbaked 9-inch pie crust (see p. 156)

4 eggs (ok to omit 2 of the yolks)

¼ to ⅓ cup brown sugar or honey

1 cup yogurt

1 tsp. vanilla extract

½ tsp. cinnamon

¼ tsp. salt

> OPTIONAL VARIATIONS:
> • Replace the sugar or honey with real maple syrup.
> • Replace the apples with sliced peaches or pitted, halved dark cherries.
> • Sprinkle a small handful of chopped nuts on top.

1) Preheat oven to 375°F.

2) Spread the apple slices evenly over the unbaked pie crust.

3) Combine all remaining ingredients in a food processor or blender and whip until frothy. Pour this custard over the apples.

4) Bake for 45 minutes, or until solid in the center. Cool for at least 1 hour before slicing. This pie tastes best at room temperature or cold.

20 minutes to prepare
(including crust);
50 minutes to bake

No-Fault Pumpkin Pie

FILLING:

2 cups cooked, puréed pumpkin or squash
   (Canned pumpkin is fine)
¼ cup white sugar
¼ cup brown sugar
2 Tbs. molasses
½ tsp. ground cloves or allspice
2 tsp. cinnamon
2 tsp. powdered ginger
¾ tsp. salt
2 beaten eggs
1 cup evaporated milk (lowfat OK)
1 unbaked 9-inch pie crust (recipe on p. 156)

OPTIONAL TOPPINGS:
whipped cream with a little sugar and rum
whipped cream with a little sugar and vanilla extract
vanilla ice cream

1) Preheat oven to 375°F.
2) Place pumpkin or squash purée in a medium-sized bowl, and add
   all other filling ingredients. Beat until smooth.
3) Spread into the pie crust and bake at 375°F for 10 minutes. Turn
   the oven down to 350°F, and bake another 40 minutes, or until
   the pie is firm in the center when shaken lightly.
4) Cool at least to room temperature before serving. This pie tastes
   very good chilled, with rum- or vanilla-spiked whipped cream, or
   some high-quality vanilla ice cream.

Maple-Walnut Pie

Delicious — and very easy!

Preparation time:
20 minutes

Baking time:
30 minutes

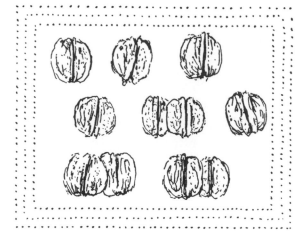

Yield:
about 6
servings

4 large eggs
3/4 cup real maple syrup
2 Tbs. lemon juice
1/4 to 1/2 tsp. cinnamon (to taste)
1 1/2 tsp. vanilla extract
1/4 tsp. salt
2 cups chopped walnuts
1 unbaked 9-inch pie crust (p. 156)
OPTIONAL: whipped cream, for the top

1) Preheat oven to 375°F.

2) Beat together all ingredients, except walnuts and pie crust, until light and frothy.

3) Spread the walnuts into the unbaked crust. Pour in the batter.

4) Bake for 30 minutes or until solid in the center. Remove from oven and allow to cool for at least 30 minutes before serving.

5) Serve warm, at room temperature, or cold, with or without whipped cream.

Crunchy-Top Peach Pie

Preparation time: about 40 minutes

Baking time: about another 40 minutes

Yield: 6 servings

Make this at the height of peach season, with the finest, ripest peaches available. Or, you can freeze some of those same fine, ripe peaches (peel and slice them first; spread on a tray and freeze, then transfer to a plastic bag, seal, and store in the freezer), and surprise everyone with this delightful pie in November.

If you have access to some equally fine and ripe apricots, they will work equally well.

6 cups sliced ripe peaches
1/4 to 1/3 cup sugar
3 Tbs. fresh lemon juice
3 Tbs. flour
1 tsp. cinnamon
a few dashes of nutmeg
1 unbaked 9-inch pie crust (p. 156)

TOPPING:
2 cups rolled oats
1/4 cup flour
1/2 tsp. salt
1/2 tsp. cinnamon
1/2 cup minced almonds
3 Tbs. brown sugar
5 Tbs. melted butter

POSSIBLE ACCOMPANIMENTS:
ice cream (recommended: vanilla, almond, or amaretto)
whipped cream
nothing at all

1) Preheat oven to 400°F.

2) Place peaches in a medium-sized bowl and sprinkle with sugar and lemon juice.

3) Combine 3 Tbs. flour and spices, and sprinkle this into the peaches. Mix gently but thoroughly. Spread this filling into the unbaked crust.

4) Combine topping ingredients in the same bowl (no need to wash it first), and mix well. Apply the topping evenly over the top, patting it firmly into place.

5) Bake for 10 minutes at 400°F, then turn the oven down to 375°F and bake for about 30 minutes more. Serve warm or cold, with ice cream or whipped cream, or just plain.

REAL BLUEBERRY PIE

About 1¼ hours
to prepare
(including baking)

Yield:
4 to 6
servings

1 <u>double</u> recipe pie crust (p. 156)
extra flour for handling the dough

6 cups blueberries (fresh or frozen/defrosted)
2 tsp. grated lemon rind
2 Tbs. fresh lemon juice
³⁄₄ cup sugar
6 Tbs. flour

1) Preheat oven to 375°F.

2) Make a double recipe of pie crust dough, and divide it into
   2 pieces, one slightly larger than the other. Lightly sprinkle a
   clean work surface with flour, and roll out the larger piece
   until it becomes a circle large enough to fit a 9-inch pie pan.
   Fit it into the pan, building it up slightly at the edges.

3) Now roll out the smaller piece of dough to a thin circle. Cut
   it into narrow strips (about ¼ inch wide), and gently set them aside

4) Place the berries in a medium-sized bowl, and sprinkle them
   with all the remaining ingredients. Toss very gently until the
   berries are evenly coated.

5) Pour the berry mixture into the crust, and decorate the top
   with the strips of dough in a criss-cross pattern.

6) Place the pie pan on a tray, and bake in the bottom half of
   the oven for 45 minutes, or until the filling is bubbly around
   the edges and the crust is lightly browned. Cool for at least
   15 minutes before serving.

Berry Sauce

Lovely, light, and easy, this sauce consists purely of berries, lightly sweetened and sieved to smoothness. Serve it as an elegant complement to many other desserts. It is incredibly good on vanilla ice cream with pieces of bittersweet chocolate on top.

This sauce can also be made with frozen unsweetened berries. Look for them in the supermarket. They usually come in sealed plastic bags.

1 cup fresh (or frozen, defrosted) berries
  (rasp-, black-, or straw-)
1 to 2 Tbs. sugar
a few drops of fresh lemon or lime juice

1) Place all ingredients in a blender or food processor, and purée.
2) Strain through a fine sieve to separate out and discard the seeds. Taste to adjust sugar and lemon juice.
3) Transfer to a container, cover tightly, and refrigerate. This sauce keeps very well for a week or longer.

Berry Sorbet or Ice

Try pairing Berry Sorbet or Ice with Meringues (p.197), to make an even more wonderful, equally nonfat treat.

1) Make Berry Sauce as described above.
2) Place the sauce in an ice cream maker, and follow the instructions for your particular machine.

If you are not the proud owner of an ice cream maker (I've never owned one myself), you can make Berry Ice:

Make Berry Sauce, place it in a tightly covered container; put it in the freezer for 30 minutes. Take it out and stir, then return it to the freezer for another 30 minutes. This would be an ideal time to serve it, but if you must wait longer, keep it frozen until about 20 minutes before serving time. Let it sit at room temperature for those 20 minutes, and stir before serving.

Ricotta Cake
~Italian-style cheesecake~

15 minutes to prepare;
50 minutes to bake

Yield: about 8 servings

Simple and plain, but full of soul.

A little soft butter for the pan
A little flour for the pan
2 lbs. (or 2 15-oz. containers) ricotta cheese
2 or 3 large eggs
2/3 cup sugar
1/3 cup flour
1 Tbs. vanilla extract
1/2 tsp. almond extract
1/2 tsp. salt
1 Tbs. grated lemon rind
3 Tbs. fresh lemon juice
OPTIONAL TOPPINGS: Fresh berries
                   Berry Sauce (p. 207)

1) Preheat oven to 350°F. Butter the bottom of a 9-inch springform pan, and dust it lightly with flour.

2) Place the ricotta, eggs, sugar, flour, vanilla and almond extracts, salt, lemon rind, and lemon juice in a food processor, and whip everything together until smooth. (Or put everything in a large bowl and beat with an electric mixer until smooth.)

3) Pour the batter into the prepared pan, and spread it into place.

4) Bake in the center of the oven for 50 minutes, or until solid in the center. Cool completely, then chill until cold.
Serve with fresh berries or Berry Sauce.

Montana's Mom's Dynamite Cheesecake

"Loved by millions from coast to coast" —Montana

Preparation time: 15 minutes

Baking time: 25 minutes, then
   a cooling period, then
   8 minutes more

Yield: enough
for 8 to 10

Basic cheesecake: unadorned and unabashed.

Make it a day ahead, so it will have plenty of time to set.

NOTE: Use a food processor or blender to make the graham cracker crumbs.

CRUST:

2 cups graham cracker crumbs
½ stick butter, melted

~Combine, and press firmly into the bottom of a 10-inch springform pan.

FILLING:

16 oz. (2 packages) cream cheese, softened   1½ tsp. vanilla extract
⅓ cup sugar   3 Tbs. lemon juice
4 eggs   ½ tsp. lemon rind

1) Preheat oven to 375°F.
2) Beat all filling ingredients together until smooth.
3) Pour onto crust and bake for 25 minutes, or until set. Remove from oven and cool to room temperature. You will need the oven again, so you can either leave it on, or reheat it.

TOPPING:

1½ cups sour cream
3 Tbs. sugar
½ tsp. vanilla extract

1) Reheat oven to 375°F.
2) Blend topping ingredients well, and pour on top of cooled cake.
3) Bake for 8 minutes. Remove from oven and cool to room temperature, then cover tightly (still in the pan) and chill at least 12 hours.

YOGURT · CREAM CHEESE PIE

CRUST:

2 heaping cups crushed graham crackers
½ tsp. cinnamon
½ cup (1 stick) butter, melted

Combine the crumbs and cinnamon in a bowl, and pour in the melted butter. Stir to combine, then pat the mixture into a 9-inch pie pan, building an even wall up the sides, and forming a nice ridge around the edge. Set aside.

FILLING:

16 oz. (2 packages) cream cheese, softened
1 cup plain Greek yogurt
½ cup mild-flavored honey (or real maple syrup, or sugar)
1 Tbs. vanilla extract

Place everything in a medium-large bowl, and beat with an electric mixer until uniform. Transfer to the crust, spreading it into place and smoothing the top.

Chill until very cold ~ at least 3 hours.

Enjoy this opportunity to feature a delicious, mild-flavored artisan honey, which goes beautifully with the tart cream cheese and yogurt. You can also use real maple syrup or sugar. (The filling will be slightly softer.)

Caribbean Dream Pie

About 40 minutes
to prepare- plus
time to chill

Yield: 1
rich
9-inch pie

SWEET CRUMB CRUST:

2 cups crushed graham crackers or ginger snaps (easily
    done in a food processor)
½ cup shredded unsweetened coconut (optional. If you prefer,
  you can substitute another ½ cup crushed
  graham crackers or ginger snaps.)
¼ cup finely minced pecans
6 Tbs. butter, melted

1) Preheat oven to 350°F.
2) Combine all ingredients and mix well. Press the mixture firmly
into the bottom and sides of a 9-inch pie pan, building a handsome
½-inch ridge around the edge. You will have more than enough to
fill the pie pan ~ sprinkle the rest in another pan. Place both in the
oven, and bake for 10 minutes. Remove from the oven and cool
completely.

FILLING:

1 14- or 15-oz. can sweetened condensed milk
1 Tbs. grated lime rind
½ cup plus 1 Tbs. fresh lime juice
2 bananas, peeled and sliced
½ a ripe mango, peeled and sliced (or chopped)

1) Pour the milk into a medium-sized bowl.

2) Add the grated rind and juice, and whisk for a few minutes
until the milk thickens.

3) Layer the banana and mango slices in the baked, cooled crust.
Pour the thickened milk mixture over the fruit, spreading it
into place. Sprinkle the top with extra crumb mixture, and chill
until cold. Serve cold.

Ginger-Brandy Cheesecake

Preparation time: 20 minutes

Baking time: 40 minutes

Yield: 8 to 10 servings

I. CRUST: 2 cups ginger snap crumbs (make them in a food processor or a blender. Or the old-fashioned way, with a rolling pin)

5 Tbs. melted butter

Mix together well. Press firmly into the bottom of a 10-inch springform pan.

II. FILLING: 12 oz. (1½ packages) cream cheese, softened (lowfat OK)

1½ cups sour cream or yogurt (or a combination)

4 eggs (some or all yolks can be omitted)

¼ cup honey or sugar (or, to taste)

¼ cup brandy

2 Tbs. finely grated fresh ginger

a dash of salt

Wild Ginger

1) Preheat oven to 350°F.

2) Whip everything together until very smooth. Taste to adjust sweetening.

3) Pour onto the crust in the springform pan. Bake for 40 minutes, or until the center is firm to the touch and the edges are slightly brown. Cool completely before removing the rim of the pan and glazing.

III. GLAZE: 2 Tbs. cornstarch

¾ cup orange juice

2 Tbs. honey or sugar

1 Tbs. brandy

½ tsp. orange rind

optional: candied ginger, cut into thin strips

1) Place cornstarch in a small saucepan. Whisk in the orange juice.

2) Cook over medium heat, whisking constantly, until smooth and glossy (about 5 minutes).

3) Remove from heat, and whisk in the remaining ingredients, except the candied ginger. Pour the hot glaze onto the cooled cheesecake, spreading it evenly. If desired, decorate in an expansive pattern with strips of candied ginger. Chill thoroughly before serving.

· · · MOOSEWOOD FUDGE BROWNIES · · ·

On a brownie-intensity scale of 1 to 10, these are about an 11; in other words, not for the faint-hearted. You should probably have some good vanilla or coffee ice cream on hand, or you'll find yourself running out to the store to get some as soon as you take a bite, and this will rudely interrupt your dessert hour.

butter for the pan
5 oz. (5 squares) unsweetened chocolate
½ lb. (2 sticks) butter, softened
1¾ cups (packed) light brown sugar (white sugar also OK)
5 eggs
1½ tsp. vanilla extract
1 cup flour (use ¾ cup for fudgier brownies)
MANY OPTIONAL EMBELLISHMENTS:
1 cup chopped walnuts or pecans
1 tsp. freshly grated orange rind
½ tsp. cinnamon
a small ripe banana, mashed
2 to 4 Tbs. strong black coffee
1 cup semisweet chocolate chips
OR anything else you might think of
OR, for purists, none of the above

1) Butter a 9 X 13-inch baking pan. Preheat oven to 350°F.
2) Gently melt the chocolate. Let it cool for about 10 minutes.
3) Cream the butter and sugar in a medium-sized bowl until light and fluffy.
4) Add the eggs, one at a time, beating well after each. Stir in the vanilla.
5) Stir constantly as you drizzle in the melted chocolate. After all the chocolate is in, beat well for a minute or two.
6) Stir in flour and possible embellishments. Mix just enough to blend thoroughly.
7) Spread the batter into the prepared pan. Bake 20 to 25 minutes, or until a knife inserted into the center comes out clean. Cut into squares while still hot, then allow to cool for at least 10 minutes, if you can wait that long.

Iced Carob Brownies

If you think of carob as itself and not as a chocolate substitute, you'll appreciate these lovely brownies even more than you would anyway.

butter for the pan
½ cup (1 stick) melted butter or margarine
¼ cup carob powder
2 eggs
½ cup (packed) light brown sugar
1 tsp. vanilla extract
¼ cup water
1 cup flour
1 tsp. baking powder
¼ tsp. salt
½ cup raisins or currants
½ cup finely chopped walnuts
optional: a dash or two of cinnamon and/or allspice

1) Preheat oven to 350°F. Butter an 8-inch square pan.

2) Beat together butter, carob, eggs, sugar, and vanilla in a medium-sized bowl. Stir in the water.

3) Sift together flour, baking powder, and salt. Stir this into the first mixture along with raisins, nuts, and optional spices. Mix just enough to blend thoroughly.

4) Spread into the prepared pan, and bake 20 to 25 minutes, or until a probe comes out clean. Cool completely before icing.

. . . .

ICING: ¼ cup carob powder
        8 oz. (1 package) cream cheese, softened
        ¼ cup powdered sugar
        ½ tsp. vanilla

Beat everything together until very smooth. Spread on top of the cooled brownies.

LEMON MOUSSE

Ethereal, yet it packs a tangy punch. Serve Lemon Mousse by itself or topped with Berry Sauce (p. 207). It also goes beautifully served in tandem with many different cakes, especially Ukrainian Poppy Seed Cake (p. 189).

Lemon Mousse will keep well for several days if tightly covered and refrigerated.

¼ cup cornstarch
½ cup sugar
½ cup freshly squeezed lemon juice
½ cup water
1 tsp. grated lemon rind
2 egg whites, at room temperature
½ pint heavy cream
OPTIONAL VARIATIONS:
1 cup berries or sliced peaches
orange rind, instead of lemon

1) Place cornstarch and sugar in a small saucepan. Add lemon juice and water and whisk until smooth.

2) Cook, whisking constantly, over medium heat until thick (5 to 8 minutes). Remove from heat, transfer to a medium-sized bowl, and stir in the lemon rind. Let cool to room temperature.

3) Place the egg whites in a medium-sized mixing bowl and beat at high speed with an electric mixer until stiff but not dry. Fold this into the lemon mixture, cover tightly, and chill at least 1 hour (longer = also ok).

4) Without cleaning the beaters, whip the cream until it is firm but still fluffy. Fold this into the mousse (add optional berries or peaches at this point), cover tightly again, and chill until serving time.

♪♪ DANISH CHERRIES ♪♪

Make this delicious, beautiful, and very simple stovetop dessert well in advance OR right before serving. You can get fine results from frozen cherries (they come pitted and unsweetened in sealed plastic bags), if fresh are unavailable. No need to defrost before using.

NOTES: ♪ To blanch almonds, place them in a colander over a sink. Pour boiling water over them, and rub off the skins. Cut vertically with a sharp knife to sliver them.

♪ To whip ricotta, beat it vigorously with a whisk, or at high speed with an electric mixer.

4 cups pitted cherries
1½ Tbs. cornstarch
3 to 4 Tbs. sugar
¼ cup lemon juice
½ tsp. grated lemon rind
¾ tsp. almond extract
OPTIONAL: ½ cup blanched, slivered almonds
TOPPINGS: whipped cream
        or
        whipped ricotta cheese   } with a few blanched,
        or   slivered almonds
        plain yogurt   folded in

1) Place cherries in a heavy medium-sized saucepan, and cook over medium heat, covered, for 10 minutes.

2) Meanwhile, combine cornstarch and sugar in a small bowl. Add lemon juice and whisk until smooth. Stir this into the hot cherries, and cook over medium heat, stirring frequently, until thick (5 to 8 minutes).

3) Remove from heat and stir in lemon rind, almond extract, and slivered almonds. Serve hot, warm, room temperature, or cold, topped with whipped cream, whipped ricotta, or yogurt.

Fruited Yogurt Desserts

Almost any combination of fruit and yogurt will taste delicious - and make a filling dessert. Here are a few suggestions. Combine as close to serving time as possible.

I.

3 cups plain yogurt
1 cup fresh blueberries
1 cup seedless grapes
1 cup pitted, halved cherries
sugar, maple syrup, or honey
~to taste

Combine and chill.

II.

3 cups plain yogurt
1 cup fresh strawberries, halved
1 to 2 medium-sized ripe
   peaches, sliced
1 perfectly ripe banana, sliced
sugar, honey, or maple syrup
~to taste

Combine and chill.

III.

3 cups plain yogurt
1 to 2 medium-sized apples,
   grated
½ cup lightly toasted minced
   almonds
a dash of cinnamon
sugar, maple syrup, or honey
~to taste

Combine and chill.

INDEX

P

In 1974, Mollie Katzen hand-wrote, illustrated, and locally published a spiral-bound notebook of recipes for vegetarian dishes inspired by those she and fellow cooks served at their small restaurant in Ithaca, NY. Several iterations and millions of copies later, the *Moosewood Cookbook* has become one of the most influential and beloved cookbooks of all time—listed by the *New York Times* as one of the best-selling cookbooks in history, inducted into the James Beard Award Cookbook Hall of Fame, and coined a Cookbook Classic by the International Association of Culinary Professionals. Mollie's *Moosewood Cookbook* has inspired generations to fall in love with plant-based home cooking, and, on the fortieth anniversary of that initial booklet, continues to be a seminal, timely, and wholly personal work. With a new introduction by Mollie, this commemorative edition will be a cornerstone for any cookbook collection that long-time fans and those just discovering *Moosewood* will treasure.

MOLLIE KATZEN is one of the best-selling cookbook authors of all time. Named by *Health Magazine* as one of the "five women who changed the way we eat," she is widely credited with helping to move plant-based cuisine from the fringe to the center of the American dinner plate. Her twelve titles include the classic *Enchanted Broccoli Forest*, a trilogy of cookbooks for children (dubbed "the gold standard of children's cookbooks" by the *New York Times*), and the award-winning *The Heart of the Plate: Vegetarian Recipes for a New Generation*. Mollie lives in Northern California.